NATURAL HOUSEKEEPING

NATURAL HOUSEKEEPING

Rediscovered Recipes for Home Care

BEVERLY PAGRAM

Gaia Books Limited

A GAIA ORIGINAL

Books from Gaia celebrate the vision of Gaia, the self-sustaining living Earth, and seek to help its readers live in greater personal and planetary harmony.

Editorial	Jo Godfrey Wood
	Clare Stewart
Design	Sara Mathews
Photography	Iain Bagwell
Managing Editor	Pip Morgan
Production	Lyn Kirby
Direction	Patrick Nugent

® This is a Registered Trade Mark of Gaia Books Limited

First published in the United Kingdom in 1997 by
Gaia Books Ltd, 66 Charlotte St, London W1P 1LR
and 20 High St, Stroud, Glos GL5 1AS

ISBN 1-85675-024-8 (H/B)
ISBN 1-85675-034-5 (P/B)

A catalogue record of this book is available from the British Library.

Printed and bound in Hong Kong

Colour separation by Fotographics, London/Hong Kong

10 9 8 7 6 5 4 3 2 1

DEDICATION

For my grandmother, Elizabeth Beatrice:
ninety-two and
still making patchwork squares and pickles.

CONTENTS

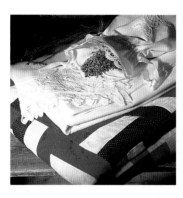

INTRODUCTION

> *"Why, I wouldn't swap this little shack
> here for th'finest house in New York.
> I wouldn't do it. That's just the way I feel."*
>
> 76-YEAR-OLD MOTHER-OF-TWELVE MRS MAUDE SHOPE OF
>
> NORTH CAROLINA, INTERVIEWED IN FOXFIRE TWO, 1973

This book is about rediscovering household wisdoms and codes of self-sufficiency from the past and using them to forge a healthier, more creative future for ourselves and our descendants.

If you dream about ending your dependence on the supermarket and chemist, and if you like making things, you will find in the following chapters many fascinating, ecologically-sound antique domestic hints, as well as imaginative ways to make your dwelling, whether it be a tiny apartment, a compact cottage, or a palatial house, look and smell like a real home.

Many of these tips have been gleaned from "household receipt" record and recipe books hand-written by genteel English, American, and Australian countrywomen from the 17th to the late 19th century. Others come from shabby, much-used kitchen notebooks that were often the only personal record of the lives of "ordinary" women of quite staggering stamina and innovative powers. Others still come from the "use what's in your storecupboard" household encyclopedias and advice manuals that proliferated in England, Europe, and the New World right up until the advent of television, when they were labelled "quaint old wives' tales" and, for the most part, discarded.

Unfinished quilts have always denoted spinster-hood and it has always been thought that a woman who completes a quilt without assistance will never be married.

These days women, whether working wives or mothers or both, have a multiplicity of challenging roles, but women 300, or even 100, years ago had to be even more adept at juggling the chores. In any one day a woman might be called upon to be a child-carer, cook, gardener, cleaner (who had to make her own cleaning potions since they were not available to be purchased in shops), home-physician, apothecary, perfumer, and cosmetician. Above all she would be skilled in "wortcunning", otherwise known as herbalism.

It was on the back of this botanical study that her huge storehouse of knowledge, from healing to home-spinning to animal husbandry, rested completely. It is indeed fair to say that without the extensive knowledge of herbalism (including borrowed Native American plantcraft) practised assiduously by Canadian and American colonial wives, successful settlement would have been well nigh impossible.

Many people in our post-industrial western society have wearied of the galloping consumerism and convenience lifestyle that threaten to engulf us, and are looking for both a sense of fulfil-ment and a "spirit of place". They want their homes to be cen-tres of emotional regeneration – sanctuaries from the hustle and bustle of the workaday world.

The folkloric and historical/herbal background to some of these domestic recipes lifts them out of the realms of the mundane and into the arcane. In performing some of the hauntingly fra-grant age-old rituals in this book – making musky pot-pourri and creamy beeswax floor polish for example – you can feel part of a female historical continuum that is uniquely satisfying and empowering.

Espousing thrift and self-reliance in caring for your domain with your home-made non-toxic products is not just about rural nostalgia; and certainly not about the rehabilitation of unwelcome drudgery. It's about saying a firm "no" to manipulative advertising campaigns and multinational chemical industries.

You will be astonished at how brilliantly, almost miraculously, some of the ordinary storecupboard ingredients, such as lemon juice and normal baking soda, work as cleansers, and wonder at how quickly you come to rely on the soothing smell of lavender on your bed-linen. Experiment with the aromatic recipes (although you must never use essential oils directly on your skin), and use them as a springboard for your imagination and your individuality.

> *"Plant me a garden to heal the heart,*
> *Balm for joy, and the sweet violet…*
> *Plant me a garden to heal the soul,*
> *A garden of peace and tranquility,*
> *Soothéd with the scent of lavender."*
> ELIZABETHAN SONG

You won't actually spend more time looking after your home if you adopt some of these traditional methods, you'll just have fewer lurid plastic bottles under the sink and more money in your purse!

Simplified shopping means that you will start to re-think the things you throw away. You will start to recycle bottles and jars and start to look forward to seeing and smelling your hand-labelled home produce in them (which will no doubt be coveted as gifts by your family, friends, and neighbours!).

Growing and harvesting your own herbs and using them and herbal essential oils in highly practical applications may make you feel in harmony with the natural world. But it is also important to see these recipes against their vivid backstory of 5000 years of association with the mysterious "other" world – that of superstition, myth, and legend.

Ancient Egyptians used herbs liberally for religious and everyday purposes. Continuing the tradition, the rosemary-bedecked Ancient Greeks scented their floors with wild violets, while the Romans were partial to sitting out in the "hortus", the herb-planted courtyard.

> *"Here's pennyroyal and marigolds,*
> *Come buy my nettletops!*
> *Here's watercresses and scurveygrass,*
> *Come buy my sage of virtue, ho!*
> *Come buy my wormwood and mugworts,*
> *Here's all fine herbs of every sort..."*
> STREET-CRY OF THE HERBWOMEN

In late medieval times the Crusaders brought back to England a multitude of new exotic herbs, resins, spices, and flowers from the East – all with their own existing ancient mythologies. By Renaissance times in Europe a complex superstitous belief system had sprung up around herbs, all of which were believed to have magical powers linked to the stars and the zodiac.

Other, supernaturally-based domestic folk-customs, beliefs and omens, described by Goethe as "the poetry of life", survive to this day in urban and urbane society, far removed from the original rural divinations and fertility festivals – some of which date back to the all-powerful Mother Goddess of prehistory – that spawned them.

Therefore, alongside the main "practical" text in this book you will find a international miscellany of superstitions, poetic quotes, nonsensical archaic advice, and difficult but spell-binding venerable "receipts". All of which, I hope, entertain and/or inspire you as you browse though your very own personal heritage of household folk recipes.

DISCLAIMER

Some of the processes in this book could be dangerous if tried by children, or without due care and attention. All herbal products, soaps and cleaners need to be kept out of the reach of children at all times.

If you are pregnant, or suffer from any allergic condition whatsoever, you must seek the advice of a qualified aromatherapist before using any essential oils. Store essential oils in a cool, dark place, out of the reach of children.

The P O R C H & H A L L

> " 'Is there anybody there?' said the Traveller,
> Knocking on the moonlit door."
>
> THE LISTENERS, WALTER DE LA MARE

The porch, front door, and hall are important points of transition between the outside world and the private sanctuary of the family home. They are significant in the myth and folklore of all cultures around the world and are celebrated thoroughly in rites and rituals.

Lucky you are indeed if you have a porch around your front door. In Europe this feature is probably little more than an extended door surround; a windbreak to house plants and a useful space for leaving muddy boots and shoes. But in the United States and Australia porches can be large enough to serve as an additional room, to sit out on in calming rocking chairs during long hot afternoons, and even to sleep on in high summer.

The door's real and symbolic value in keeping out the elements and unwanted visitors, real and of the spirit world, reveals itself in the decorations and lore it has accrued over the centuries. In Sumatra dragons and mythical creatures are still carved around it, while in parts of Bavaria traditional wooden door-guardian "cherubs" are enjoying a revival. Many British people still hang a horseshoe over the door-lintel, but too few are aware that the shoe, the sign of the pagan horse-goddess Epona, must have the two ends pointing upward, otherwise the good luck just falls out!

*"Where rosemary
flourishes the
woman rules."*

ANON.

Chinese Feng Shui principles extend into the realms of numerology. Certain house numbers are believed to be very lucky. One of the most favoured is thirteen, which is associated with the Lord Buddha. However, in the Western world, the number thirteen is universally thought to be unlucky because there were thirteen guests present at the Last Supper, and because there are always thirteen members gathered at a meeting of a witches' coven.

The Amish people of Pennsylvania still paint mystical symbols on their doorposts, while many old Dutch houses of that region still boast red anti-witch hex signs. Native Americans of all the various tribes traditionally hang amulets at the entrances to their lodges and tipis, while in parts of Spain, Portugal, and Tunisia a "magical" painted line of intense blue surrounds and protects all doorways and windows.

The threshold itself – neither in nor out of the house – has always been thought of as a dangerous place. Under many ancient doorsteps throughout Europe are buried open scissors, a symbolic reminder of the pre-Roman times when iron was regarded to be a sacred metal. The universal custom of carrying the new bride over the threshold dates from the times when it was believed that her fertility might be harmed by malignant threshold gremlins.

The hall is the next place to affect the senses of the visitor after the all-important approach to the façade of the house and the porch and door. This is a significant transitional space, and one whose mood and character is too often neglected by the house-holders in their haste to move on to the main rooms.

(Previous page)
**"And I polished up
the handle of the
big front door."**

H.M.S.PINAFORE,

SIR W. S. GILBERT

A traditionally welcoming hall offers tantalizing and mysterious glimpses of other rooms through its open doors. Its special scents gently assail the senses of the visitor with wafts of lavender polish mingled with seasonal flowers and spicy pomanders or pot-pourri on the hall table. "What is that lovely smell?" should be an oft-heard visitors' question.

The concept of the hall dates back to baronial castles, where visitors stepped straight into a gigantic hall-living room warmed by a vast fire-place. A hall was of course a luxury not always enjoyed by working-class Europeans or colonial settlers. Nevertheless, houseproud thrifty Australian wives made natty doormats out of flour sacks and car tyre inner tubes to impress their guests with, while many a backwoods log cabin in America fabricated a tiny "hall" out of hanging quilts.

Our spirits sink or are uplifted whenever we step into the hall of someone's home. Great expanses of chemically treated acrylic carpet may not look or feel inviting, but flagstones and terra-cotta tiles with wool or cotton scatter rugs are both tactile and healthy. So are wooden floors and stairs, which, if new, should ideally be constructed from hardwood or softwood that comes from a sustainable source.

For those who look at their tiny cramped hall and despair, remember that amazing illusions of space and light can be created by the clever use of mirrors, and that a *trompe l'oeil* mural of trees and flowers can give even the most ordinary urban vestibule instant country charm.

Herbs have long been grown around the front door or on the porch and their significance since pre-Christian times in all aspects of homely life – as vital ingredients in cooking, in physic, and in religious rituals of all kinds, as well as in cleansing and beautifying the house – makes them a highly appropriate frame for any front door.

Some people have their herb garden at the back of the house as part of a kitchen garden potager, but to my mind that is to deny onself and one's guests the inimitable scented welcome provided by sun-warmed or rain-washed herbs and their traditional companions – romantically billowing cottage-style roses. Occasions and friendships can be remembered in the exchange and gift of plants, cuttings, or seeds as the guests take their leave.

"All rising to great place is by a winding stair."

"OF GREAT PLACE", ESSAY, BACON, 1625

In medieval illustrations "herbers", as herb-gardens were called, were grand affairs transversed by "covert alleys" of plaited willow and juniper, while in Tudor and Renaissance times the importance of such gardens was emphasized by the geometric complexity of their "knot" designs. However, in this day and age, even someone with a pocket-sized plot can create a containerized "living history" dooryard garden which is both an escapist's fragrant "secret" bower and a useful household apothecary allotment.

Planting a herb garden was one of the first things our ancestors did when they moved house. Paper-twists of herb-seed were among the minimalist luggage of America's first colonists, while a heady mix of nostalgia and practical necessity made Australian pioneer farmer's wives insist that some of the precious water for the crops be used on the valiant English herbs that had emigrated with them all the way across the world.

In times gone by some herbs and plants were thought to have supernatural powers and magical intentions, therefore planting them adjacent to the house was not only for their usefulness but to court good luck or avert disaster. Of the bay tree, for example, Culpeper wrote that "it resisteth witchcraft very potently", while since the Roman era people have grown house-leeks on their roofs to protect the dwelling from the perils of thunder and lightning.

It was an ancient English custom for brides to take a piece of rosemary from their bridal hair-wreath and plant it outside the door before they entered their new home.

In England and Europe in times of old, a herbalist, a "white witch", was known by the pot of the ancient Eurasian herb mugwort, also known as cronewort, that she kept by her front door. Mugwort was thought to have supernatural powers.

Herbs have been grown on balconies since the "hanging gardens" of Babylon. Analysis of the volcanic ash and debris at

"Smell is the sense of the imagination."

JEAN-JACQUES ROUSSEAU

Pompeii reveals that there herbs were grown in courtyards in giant urns. Even the jaded Spanish conquistadores were impressed by the intricate containerized herbal roof gardens cultivated by the Aztecs.

THE INDOOR HERB GARDEN

Although the activity of herb-growing is usually thought of as being appropriate only for cottage gardens, you can grow enough ordinary household herbs for your everyday needs on a tiny town balcony, or even indoors in an apartment on a sunny window-sill. The latter can be cunningly "enlarged" with the aid of pieces of simple garden trellis, shelves, and hanging baskets, or even a simple external wooden window greenhouse. A window facing south is the ideal choice, but either east or west are perfectly acceptable, too.

Herbs cultivated inside have a longer growing season, and of course they give the room a delightful odour. A compatible group of plants living in close proximity create a mutually beneficial micro-climate.

Herbs, indeed all indoor and pot plants, do not react well to well-meant but injurious overwatering – especially in the dormant winter season. What they do like is well-drained compost with broken crocks or a handful of small stones in the bottom of the pot, and being part of a self-contained eco-system of plants arranged on smooth, rounded pebbles. If the main dish is regularly given a water top-up (to just below the level of the plant pots), the humidity of your room, as well as its air quality, will be vastly improved and the herbs will remain much healthier for far longer.

In hot weather many plants like a gentle tepid spray with a water mister. This is particularly important in urban areas where the herbs, like humans, can suffer from pollutant-stress. The high nitrogen content of comfrey leaves means that they are an excellent organic fertilizer. Two-day-old comfrey tea is an excellent nutritious feed to give to your herbs.

> *"In March and in April,*
> *from morning to night*
> *In sowing and setting, good housewives delight*
> *To have in a garden, or other like plot*
> *To physic their house, or to furnish their pot."*
>
> FIVE HUNDRED POINTES OF GOOD HUSBANDRIE,
>
> THOMAS TUSSER, 1573

Sowing from seed is highly rewarding, but don't forget to label the pots and seed-trays and read the packet instructions carefully so that you know if you are expecting an annual, a biennial, or a perennial flower. Egg-boxes make good seed trays – you can break off each individual "cup" when the seedling is mature enough and plant it straight into the garden – the cardboard acts as a fertilizer. If you buy a young plant from a garden centre, check that its root system has enough leg-room for the growing season – if not, re-pot.

THE SMALL HOUSEHOLD HERB GARDEN

The American Museum at Claverton Manor, Bath, in England, has a charming miniature herb garden showing the sort of household herbs grown by colonial housewives. Centred around a bee skep, it is exemplary in its imaginative use of limited space. If you do not have the room or inclination for a herb-garden in the medieval style – long rectangular beds filled with a single herb species – you may well wish to adopt this sort of economic but eclectic planting scheme.

Diminutive fragrant herb gardens which echo the past but have a strong contemporary look can be created by the use of the wheel as a template. Some people literally use old bicycle wheels or (harder to find) cart-wheels to plant in, but most just mark out the site using a central stake and some string. Knots and formal geometric shapes require a lot of pruning to continually look good, but large circles can have wild, tumbling herb beds punctuated with paved, cobbled, or gravelled path radials – it is important to be able to actually get to your herbs without trampling the garden.

I once kept a colony of different sorts of mint in an old Victorian roll-top bath. The usual advantage of using containers of various kinds is, of course, their mobility! Urns, chimney-pots, and old sinks can be moved around the patio or courtyard accordingly to make the most of the flowering seasons of the herbs, and to chime in with your personal whims.

Don't forget to sprinkle aromatic plant seed between your paving stones for a fragrant footfall. The irrepressible mint *Mentha requienii,* which has the smallest leaves of any cultivated plant, is an ideal candidate for bursting out of cracks and crannies in a surprising, scented way.

WHAT TO GROW IN THE HOUSEHOLD GARDEN

Roses are a must, because their petals are invaluable in pot-pourri and bath-bags. The wrinkled, aromatic flowers of the cistus bush come into the same category. Then, my useful favourites list would include:

BORAGE, SOUTHERNWOOD, COSTMARY, SWEET JOE PYE, CLOVE PINK, MEADOWSWEET, SWEET WOODRUFF, HYSSOP, LAVENDER, MELILOT, PENNY-ROYAL, LADY'S BEDSTRAW, EAU DE COLOGNE MINT AND SPEARMINT, LEMON BALM, BERGAMOT, SWEET CICELY, CATNIP, MARJORAM, ANY SCENTED GERANIUMS, SORREL, SANTOLINA, SAGE, SOAPWORT, TANSY, THYME AND SWEET VIOLET.

Bay and rosemary are household essentials. In time both can make impressive fanciful topiary specimens for locations beside the front door. Fresh eucalyptus leaves also come in very handy for use in insect-repellent pot-pourri (see p.81). Some species of eucalypt are not only hardy but don't seem to mind growing in a container if they are coppiced or pollarded (see pp.136-7 for mail-order trees).

If you haven't got room for a chamomile lawn, create your own chamomile seat. Make a bottom-height raised bed with bricks, and fill it with loam-based compost with a little bonemeal

(Facing page)
"We often get in quicker by the back door than by the front."
NAPOLEON

added. You can make a seat back and arm-rests with more bricks, wood, or stone. Look in recycling centres for interesting and unusual bits and pieces, or on beaches for intriguing shapes of washed-up driftwood. Shells and broken crockery in mosaic patterns can be pressed into the damp cement between the bricks for an original effect. Plant apple-scented chamomile ("Treneague" is a robust variety), and let it establish for about three months before you sit in your balmy grotto.
(See also pp.38-40.)

THE PORCH

Before stepping in here in the winter folks usually get the worst off their footwear with a **bootscraper**. If you're not blessed with a fancy antique, make an impromptu one with a partly submerged tin bucket, North Carolina mountain folk-style. Keep **ice** from forming on the front steps by washing them with hot water in which a handful of salt has been dissolved. Marks on stone steps can be rubbed off with ordinary pumice.

Remember that highly prized **leather boots** that are exposed to wind and weather must never be dried in front of the fire or they will harden and crack. Stand them in the porch, stuffed full of newspaper to keep their shape. Regular applications of castor oil helps to waterproof leather boots.

A chain-store curtain-rod attached to the porch wall at child-height makes a good drying spot for wellington boots and over-shoes hooked over by their heels. Important, too, are child-height hooks for keeping coats and bags tidy. Never throw away old waxed jackets. The material is perfect for knee-patches for gardening trousers and coats for elderly dogs. Outgrown plastic macs can be cut up and made into schoolwork folders.

"Hoom to myn hous ful swiftly I me spedde, And in a little herber that I have, Y-benched new with turves fresshe y-grave, I bod men shulde me my couche make."
THE LEGEND OF GOOD
WOMEN, CHAUCER, 1385

On the **hat-stand**, hang sunhats decorated about the brim with garlands of sweet-smelling lavender, as worn by Elizabethan and Tudor gardeners to repel flies and uplift the spirits. Hats like these are a wonderful visual and aromatic bonus both on the hat stand and off.

An old chimney pot with a large sponge in the bottom to absorb the drips makes an unusual ornamental **umbrella stand**. It is generally thought to be inauspicious to open an umbrella indoors – a superstition imported from India, where the umbrella or sunshade was a symbol of the sun's power and was only allowed to be used by royalty.

American folk-belief states that any young woman who picks up a fallen umbrella will remain single. John Gerard recommended impromptu umbrellas made from the huge leaves of butterbur. The leaves, he said, were "of such widenesse to keepe a man's head from raine, and from the heat of the sun".

The Dictionary of Daily Wants, 1841, gives some very sound advice on the subject of umbrellas: "Umbrellas should not be kept tightly done up when not in use, as the continual pressure of the ribs on the material causes it to wear through those parts. It is prudent to keep two umbrellas, one for your own use, and one to lend in emergencies, for it is proverbial that borrowed umbrellas are never returned, or if returned, not until they are half worn out, and the immediate need for them has gone by."

DECORATE YOUR CHAMOMILE SEAT WITH SEASIDE KEEPSAKES AND COLOURFUL CROCKS (SEE FACING PAGE).

THE FRONT DOOR
Doorknockers, originally devised to protect doors from the considerable wear and tear inflicted by visitors hammering on them with sticks and sword-handles, are often formed in the shape of protective beasts such as griffons and lions, or the talismanic female hand used throughout France, Spain, and the Middle East.

When you are cleaning **brass door furniture**, a small piece of cardboard placed temporarily behind the knocker or doorknob will prevent polish smears transferring to the paintwork. Most brass responds well to lemon juice and salt applied with a soft toothbrush, rinsed off, and then buffed up with a very soft duster. A little olive oil rubbed on to the cleaned brass will keep it brighter longer. Remember not to clean it too thoroughly or it will look too bright and take on a "just-bought" appearance.

OAK POLISH

HEAT ONE LITRE (32FL OZ)
OF BEER, TWO OUNCES
(57G) OF BEESWAX AND A
TABLESPOON OF SUGAR.
WHEN THE POLISH IS COOL,
APPLY AND ALLOW TO DRY
BEFORE BUFFING TO A SHINE
WITH A SOFT DUSTER.

Front door paintwork is best refreshed with equal amounts of warm water and vinegar, with a squirt of biodegradable washing-up liquid. To keep winter draughts at bay around the front door make a thick curtain (luscious rich velvet or heavy brocade) to hang inside the door on a *portière* rod. It will give your hall a cosy medieval atmosphere. To render the curtain extra effective, interline it with unwanted old blankets. You will be surprised at the difference it makes. A **doormat** sheds its dust-load easiest if you put it face-down outside and beat it vigorously with an old tennis racquet. A sheet of strong brown paper underneath the mat catches any loose dust, for easy disposal afterwards.

THE HALL

The gentle, elegant "background" smell of home-made beeswax and lavender **floor-polish** will be one of the things that people notice subliminally as soon as they step into your house.

If you are lucky enough to have **oak stairs** and **floorboards**, use the old oak polish recipe (see left) to keep the wood supple and sweet-smelling. Plenty of elbow-grease and a soft duster brings up the grain wonderfully. Just as oak likes beer, so **slate** enjoys a nutritious drink of milk. A swift wipe with a milky cloth before you start polishing brings up the subtle sheen and patina of slate tiles like magic.

For those who feel like experimenting with polishes, many thrifty old recipes utilize melted candles, but this is really only a good idea if the stubs are unrefined beeswax, not petroleum-derived wax. Don't forget to remove the wicks.

If the **hall runner carpet** becomes muddy, rubbing with raw potato removes any residual stain that won't brush off. Damp, earthy smells can be "made faire" with a plant-spray half filled with water and four drops of essential oil. Bergamot is both anti-septic and an anti-depressant. Sweeping in between the **bannis-ter uprights** on the stairs is best done with a decorator's paint-brush or a child's brush-and-dustpan set.

In Victorian times it was common for stairs to be lined with heavy pots of scented pelargoniums for the voluminous ladies' skirts of the day to brush against.

If you have a **stair carpet**, make sure it is backed by hessian or felt, rather than foam, which is a petrochemical by-product and thus part of one of the world's most polluting and toxic industries. You can save wear and tear on your stair carpet by buying a little more than you need and folding the extra bit under the bottom stair. When the tread starts to become scuffed and worn, move the carpet up or down so that the worn areas are no longer trodden on. The old-fashioned way of fixing stair carpets and runners, with removable metal rods rather than permanently fixed carpet tacks, makes this easier to achieve and therefore a far more realistic proposition.

When we say "touch wood" we are invoking the protective Druidic power of the sacred oak tree. The carved wooden acorn that continues to adorn many stair newel-posts has the same origin – to protect the family from the "nether-world" between two floors.

The still-held belief that it is inauspicious to pass anyone on the stairs originates in the precariously narrow spiral staircases that ascended and descended castle turrets. The person coming up felt at a serious tactical disadvantage, and whatever happened neither of the stair-travellers had enough room to easily unsheath their swords.

The **hall table** is often a messy repository for family post, keys, and assorted bits and pieces. An impromptu hotel-style mail-sort system can easily be made out of a customized wine-rack fixed to the wall. This leaves the table free for an assortment of aromatherapeutic decorations.

A favourite 19th-century Devon farmhouse family receipt (see p.28) can be adapted to suit the time of year and whatever is available to be picked or gathered. Bright seasonal flowers

In Elizabethan times pomanders were originally little apple-shaped pieces of ambergris – *pommes d'ambre,* carried around the neck in a filigree ball on a chain and sniffed constantly to keep at bay the foul odours of the street.

"I have loved flowers that fade, Within whose magic tents Rich hues have marriage made With sweet unmemoried scents."
ROBERT BRIDGES

ADD A SPOONFUL OF SUGAR
TO THE WATER TO PERK UP
YOUR CUT FLOWERS.

(paper-dry), citrus peel, fir-cones, shells, and seed-pods can be added and subtracted as desired.

Citrus **pomanders** punctured with cloves are a traditional Christmas decoration and a most appealing drawer-scenting gift. Yet a large bowl of them, interspersed with lacquered gourds and squashes, makes an unusual, spicy hall table delight for any time of year, but particularly for the autumn.

Miss Tilvey's Wood Polish

¼ LITRE (8FL OZ) PURE TURPENTINE
56G (2OZ) BEESWAX
28G (1OZ) PURE SOAP, GRATED
113ML (3FL OZ) LINSEED OIL
4 DROPS ESSENTIAL OIL OF LAVENDER
2 DROPS ESSENTIAL OIL OF ROSEMARY

The waxes and turpentine can be mixed together in a double boiler or in a bowl over hot water, but keep the temperature just warm as this is an inflammable mixture. Add the essential oils when you pour the polish into a bottle. Shake well before use and apply sparingly. Buff to a gleam rather than a gloss, for safety reasons.

MISTRESS TRICKEY'S BASIC
BIDEFORD POT-POURRI

COLLECT HALF-DRIED ROSE
LEAVES (PETALS) AND LAVEN-
DER AS THEY BLOOM. PLACE
IN A JAR WITH COMMON
(NON-IODIZED) SALT. TURN
DAILY UNTIL DRY, THEN ADD
POWDERED CLOVES, ORRIS
ROOT, CINNAMON, CASSIA
BUDS, DROPS OF PATCHOULI,
AND ANY OTHER ODOROUS
INGREDIENTS AS YE SEE FIT.

Small thin-skinned oranges should be stuck all over with cloves (a knitting needle or bodkin can be used if this proves tough on the fingers), until there is no skin visible, then rolled in equal parts of orris powder (violet-scented powder from the root of the *Iris germanica var. Florentina*, used as a fixative), and cinnamon and left wrapped up in the residue in greaseproof paper for about six weeks. The pomanders will emerge quite hard and dry, and smelling delightfully of the mystic East.

Floral arrangements on the hall table will fail to emit a rank smell after a few days if you add a small piece of charcoal to the flower water. When gathering your blooms, always pick them in the early morning or evening, as those picked in full sun don't seem to last very long. Roses invariably last better if they still have the dew on them when picked, and if you crush the ends of their stems.

Most cut flowers will last longer when brought into the house if the ends of their stems are snipped. They also revive after an hour or two in a cool, dark room, resting in a bucket of lukewarm water to which one teaspoon of sugar per half litre (16fl oz) has been added. To prevent tulips from wilting and losing their petals in a warm hall, tie a piece of cotton nearly the same colour as the flower around the unfurled bud. In the depths of winter interestingly shaped branches and dried seed-heads can look spare and elegant in a clear glass vase.

It is in the hall that people often display their ornate pier glasses and antique **mirrors.** It is important that you never take the back off an old mirror to clean it, as the mercury it contains is extremely toxic. Corroded "spotted" silvering, part of the mirror's ageing process, can in fact look rather atmospheric as long as the mirror glass is actually clean. Instead, remove any dust with a soft bannister brush, then rub the surface of the mirror with a rag dabbed in either spirits of camphor (available from the pharmacist), a little neat vodka, or water in which a little starch has been dissolved. (See also p.120.)

IN COLONIAL NEW ENGLAND, MIRRORS WERE SOMETIMES WASHED WITH AN INFUSION OF ONION OR LEEK JUICE TO KEEP INSECTS FROM SETTLING ON THEM. CLEANING WITH METHYLATED SPIRIT LEAVES A VERY UNPLEASANT RESIDUAL SMELL.

*"Not many sounds in life,
and I include all urban and rural sounds,
exceed in interest a knock at the door."*
VALENTINE'S DAY, ESSAYS OF ELIA, 1823

The KITCHEN

> *"It smelled good. The whole house smelled good, with the sweet and spicy smells from the kitchen, and the smell of the hickory logs burning with clear, bright flame in the fireplace, and the smell of a clove-apple beside Grandma's mending basket on the table."*
>
> LITTLE HOUSE IN THE BIG WOODS, SET IN 1880s WISCONSIN,
> LAURA INGALLS WILDER

Throughout the ages the kitchen has been the symbolic heart of the home, the engine-room of household care and management. The cleaning and food-preparation smells of the busy kitchen evoke childhood memories for many people, and in folk-memory the kitchen represents a gravitational centre of warmth and comfort. With its strings of onions and garlic, bunches of herbs, and mysterious jars emitting interesting smells, it is a haven humming with the easy conversation of family and friends.

As we approach the new millennium and our working lives are more engulfed by modern technologies, it is often in our kitchens, surrounded by homely everyday objects, that we feel most relaxed and nurtured. This is where self-expression and emergent life philosophies often find their first voice and sometimes overlap. Creativity can manifest itself in many ways – for example in a choice of kitchen colours, textures, and patterns that reflect the landscape outside, in using waste paper to create a papier mâché bowl, in inviting nature inside with a window-sill herb garden and using its bounty to make useful and beautiful potions and pot-pourris.

The resourcefulness of our forebears relied on their being fine-tuned to the days, weeks, and months of the seasons. In the days before refrigeration and mass production the creativity of the housewife was a practical necessity, not a romantic whim. Just as her autumn pantry or larder gleamed with vividly coloured preserves, so her stillroom exuded the heady perfumes of freshly made soap, and tightly stoppered phials of attar of roses.

> *"I had often to notice the use made of fragments and small opportunities in Cranford; the rose leaves that were gathered even as they fell to make into a pot-pourri of some one who had no garden, the little bundles of lavender flowers sent to strew the drawers of some town-dweller, or to burn in the chamber of some invalid."*
>
> CRANFORD, MRS GASKELL

The household-alchemist selecting ingredients from the many tiny drawers of her "spicery cupboard" and pounding them to exotic dust with her mortar and pestle is a potent image, and one which many apartment-dwellers may think is not for them. But in fact it is not necessary to live in a 17th-century thatched cottage to recreate and use some of the excellent evergreen unguents of the past and recapture a sense of self-sufficiency. Few homes these days have a stillroom, so-called because it contained a distillation device for the manufacture of essential oils and flower essences. Today's domestic apothecary may have to make do with a safe corner of the kitchen dresser.

The current upsurge in interest in aromatherapy has revealed how important that neglected memory-jolting sense, smell, is to our well-being. The joy of the old-time recipes in this book is that they all smell wholesome and good. Once you've tried them you will probably want to experiment with different herbs and oils – the world is your olfactory oyster!

Choice is a luxury not to be wasted, and an important issue in resources of the world and eco-pollution can manifest itself in

(Previous page)
THE CAST-IRON TOP OF AN OLD COOKING RANGE LIKE THIS CAN BE KEPT SHINY BY FREQUENT APPLICATIONS OF BEESWAX, BUFFED VIGOROUSLY.

your kitchen in many ways. It can be in using a "breathing" milk-and-earth pigment paint instead of the fungicide and preservative-filled, oil-based variety; it can be in using furniture made from woods from sustainable forests; by composting household waste; by recycling as many items as possible – utilizing plastic bottles as scoops and funnels perhaps; by saving electricity in the evenings by eating by magical candle-light (ideally home-made); and by cleaning sinks and ovens with the wholesome wizardry of herbal vinegars instead of corrosive, eco-hostile chemical cocktails.

Water conservation, another important kitchen eco-issue, is as vital today as it was to the "huswife" of the 17th century. A tap dripping every second can waste nearly 600 bathfuls of water a year. A half-full dishwasher can use up to 32 litres (seven gallons) more than washing by hand. In colonial outback Australia precious water was often carried great distances in buckets fashioned from kerosene tins. There and in New England greasy floors were cleaned not with water but painstakingly scoured with silver sand.

Naturally, the emigrants from the Old World took their superstitions along with their ancient books of household receipts. Dark Age taboos about spilling salt, as well as Druidic rules about stirring a mixture "sunwise" still linger today in modern Western culture. They also borrowed liberally from the environmentally aware peoples of the New World – the Aboriginal germicides eucalyptus and tea-tree, for example, and the traditional Algonquin Indian use of pokeweed as a dye plant.

CLEANING

There is a vast, complex array of household cleansers on the market which are designed not only to eliminate dirt but to deodorize and disinfect, as well. Most of them contain chemical irritants that may be harmful, not only to us but to the environment. The effective ecological cleaning cupboard revolves around the magical triumvirate of vinegar, bicarbonate of soda, and lemon juice, assisted by essential oils and herbs.

"C-L-E-A-N, clean, verb active, to make bright, to scour."
NICHOLAS NICKLEBY,
CHARLES DICKENS, 1839

LEMON PEEL PUT IN A WARM
OVEN WILL HELP TO GET RID
OF LINGERING SMELLS.

Pure lavender oil outranks carbolic acid as a disinfectant. Three or four drops steeped in a bottle of warmed vinegar (not malt) and left to cool makes a forceful yet delightful-smelling

> *"There were few commercial cleaners on the market when I was a small child, but there was the brick board on to which dust from a fine brick was shaved with an old knife and with this and a piece of soft cloth the steel knives and forks for the table, as well as the kitchen cutlery, were scoured."*
>
> THE COUNTRY KITCHEN, SET IN SOUTH MICHIGAN, 1870s, DELLA LUTES

all-purpose cleanser. Rosemary oil, a powerful natural bactericide used in French hospitals earlier this century, can also be used the same way; as can thyme, whose thymol is an extremely potent antiseptic. You'll find that a few drops of herbal vinegar in the **washing-up water** will make the greasiest dishes sparkle, but rinse them well afterwards. Herbal vinegar, sprayed with a pump-action plant-mister on to thickly spread bicarbonate of soda, will make short work of greasy **tiles** and grimy **cupboards**. If you are cleaning inside the oven, use plain vinegar and bicarb. You can eradicate oven smells by putting some lemon peel on a tray in the warm oven. You can successfully eliminate stubborn stains on rough **wooden surfaces** such as chopping boards with lemon juice rubbed on with a nail-brush, but be careful, as it is a natural bleaching agent.

Shaker-style **tin-ware** is best cleaned with a solution of hot washing soda and water, then polished up with a piece of raw onion. In parts of rural Germany sandpapery equisetum ("horsetail") leaves – "Zinnkraut" – are still sold in markets for the traditional scouring of **pewter**. Pewter must never be polished, or it will lose its unique patina. Use old supermarket nylon fruitbags scrunched together for scouring if you can't find equisetum. Dull and dirty **copper** kettles and pans respond well

(Facing page)
*"The corn that makes
the holy bread
By which the soul
of man is fed,"*
THE EVERLASTING MERCY,
1911

to being washed with equal parts of vinegar and salt. Rinse well and burnish with a soft cloth – old socks and gloves are ideal. If you have any cookware to which the odour of fish, onions, or cabbage lingers, you can make them fresh with a sluice of hot water and plain white wine vinegar.

"Scraps of soap should be saved until there are a certain number of them. Then melt them all down and mix with some silver sand. When they begin to set, form into a ball. This is excellent for removing stains from the hands."

I HAVE A HOUSE – HOUSEHOLD KNOWLEDGE NEW AND OLD, MAY SLADE AND DIANA HAMMOND, 1950

In bygone days most households had to concoct their own **washing-up liquid**. This was often "soap jelly" (see p.126), an accumulation of the leftover soap scraps with a little boiling water poured on. If you live in a hard water area you might need a quarter of a cup of washing soda or borax (both are bio-degradable) in the rinsing water to increase the effectiveness of the soap. If used together with boiling water both borax and washing soda crystals keep **drains** sweet-smelling and grease-free. A damp cloth dipped in salt is very efficacious for **burnt pans**, but if they are really discoloured you can soak them overnight with water containing either rhubarb or sorrel. However, never put rhubarb in a copper saucepan as the potassium oxalate in the plant will discolour it. Some people who are concerned about the effect of phosphates on river wildlife choose to use one part borax to two parts baking soda in their dishwashers, with white wine vinegar as a rinse aid to prevent streaking.

Opening a **fridge** and being assailed by the smell of stale food is very off-putting. Clean the fridge with a half-and-half mixture of hot lemon juice and water and then keep it fresh by storing an opened box of bicarb in it to absorb odours. A large piece of charcoal does the same job. A couple of natural sponges in the vegetable drawer will absorb dampness and keep the veggies crisp.

Kettles full of **lime-scale** are another common kitchen revulsion focus. The old-fashioned way of getting rid of it was to keep an oyster shell in the bottom, but an ordinary marble from the playroom or nursery works just as effectively.

Dirty **windows** are rather a depressing prospect, but shop-bought cleaners often leave waxy smears. One-third of white vinegar to two-thirds water makes them sparkle, especially if they are polished with newspaper when nearly dry. In the winter you can keep frost off the outside of the windows by rubbing them with a little glycerine.

There is something very satisfying about sweeping your kitchen with an old-fashioned besom **broom**. Make one yourself by tying birch twigs, stiff stems of the broom brush, heather, or tough lavender stalks around a long stick, and drying it in a well-ventilated spot.

An old-fashioned walk-in **larder** or **pantry**, especially if it has a marble or slate cold-slab, is a kitchen treasure. Onions and potatoes keep very well here in the semi-gloom, hanging in old stockings. So do dried herbs, especially if you can acquire a many-drawered pharmaceutical-type storage cabinet for them, such as the Shakers used in their kitchens.

RECYCLING

Get the **recycling** system in your kitchen really well organized. Put all organic waste on to the compost heap and turn old newspaper into kindling (see p.64). Crush metal cans and take them to your local recycling centre. Those plastic bottles that you cannot recycle can be made easier to dispose of by filling them with boiling water. You will find that they are then soft enough to be easily squashed into a portable size.

PESTS

Insects can be a pest wherever food is stored, but there is an alternative to toxic insecticides. Cloves scattered on the shelves will deter **ants** and **mice**, so will dried mint (especially peppermint), cayenne powder, and chillis. **Flies**, **bluebottles**, and **blowflies** keep away from bunches of elder leaves, and similarly loathe tansy. Strip the stems of their leaves and hang up bunches of the tiny yellow tansy "buttons".

The summer-evocative gentle drone of insects in the garden is one thing, but how do you keep them from migrating into the house if your windows and doors aren't fitted with fly-screens?

ORIGINALLY BROOMS WERE MADE OF THE BROOM BUSH (*CYTISUS SCOPARIUS*). THIS WAS BECAUSE THEY DID NOT CATCH ALIGHT WHEN USED BY BAKERS TO SWEEP HOT ASHES. IN 17TH-CENTURY ENGLAND, HOUSEWIVES USED TO TIE PIECES OF ROSE-MARY AMONG THE TWIGS OF BROOMS TO DISPEL MALEVOLENT SPIRITS, MAINLY WITCHES, WHO WERE WONT TO STEAL BROOMS, RUB THEMSELVES WITH "FLYING OINTMENT" AND DISAPPEAR INTO THE SKY ON THEM!

> ### SHOO-FLY POT-POURRI
>
> *There's nothing worse, when the family is eating in the kitchen in summer, than everyone doing semaphore movements to keep away the wasps and flies. This table centrepiece helps:*
>
> 4 CUPS LAVENDER FLOWERS
> 2 CUPS DRIED MINT LEAVES OR SWEET JOE PYE LEAVES
> 2 CUPS DRIED LEMON VERBENA LEAVES
> ½ CUP CLOVES
> ½ CUP ORRIS POWDER
> 5 DROPS CITRONELLA OIL

On the continent of Europe many kitchens have a pot of basil or rue on the sill to deter flies, and in French country restaurants nettles may be hung at the window as an anti-wasp measure. Dried nettles are also used as a wrapping for soft cheese, apples, and pears – they have amazing preservative qualities.

"God in his wisdom made the fly, And then forgot to tell us why."
OGDEN NASH

PENNYROYAL, MENTHA PULEGIUM, IS NAMED AFTER THE LATIN WORD FOR FLEA – PULEX. FOR AS PLINY SAYS IN HIS NATURAL HISTORIE (77AD, TRANS. 1601) "THE FLOURES OF PENNYROIALL THAT BE FRESH AND NEW GATHERED, IF THEY BE BURNT MAKE A SINGULAR PERFUME TO KILL FLEAS."

A few bay leaves scattered among pulses and flours have always been the traditional English repellent for **weevils**. Diluted lavender oil is a good insect repellent which was used in French and Italian butcher's shops before the advent of chemical insecticides. Spray it near cracks between the floor and wall to make **silverfish** and **black beetles** retreat. Alas, the only cure for invading **cockroaches** is toxic "cockroach gateau" – mix equal parts of borax, molasses, and oatmeal and stuff it into their favourite crevices.

Many people have cat- or dog-beds in their kitchens. The ingredients of many commercial **flea-sprays**, however, can be highly irritating to human and animal respiratory tract alike. An alternative is to put eucalyptus or pennyroyal (fleabane) leaves under your pet's bedding, or rub a fabric pet-collar with a little tea-tree oil. For pure pleasure most cats appreciate a fabric mouse or cat's dream pillow stuffed full of catnip.

HARVESTING AND DRYING HERBS
Old herbals recommend Midsummer's Day, with its pagan associations with the summer solstice, as the best day for gathering

herbs. In fact many herbs are about to flower around then, so this is the ideal harvesting period – just as the plants are at their most beautiful. For herbs that are to be dried and stored (and with the exception of lavender most herbs wilt soon after picking unless the correct storage process is begun), choose a sunny morning after the dew has evaporated, but before the midday sun has minimized the strength of the essential oils. Do not wash them or you may diminish their properties. In England the slow bottom oven of the permanently lit range-type of stove makes an ideal controlled drying place for herbs – with the door left open to allow for water evaporation.

However, for charm and atmosphere it is hard to better the sight of bunches of herbs hanging from the rafters or an old-fashioned clothes-drying pulley (avoid hanging directly over the stove, though, as the steam will ruin them). To dry properly herbs like to be in a dark, warm, dry spot with adequate ventilation and not too much dust! Bright light destroys the oils in the herbs and leaches their colour. Tie robust plants such as lavender, feverfew, rosemary, thyme, and sage loosely with string into small bunches (not more than ten stems), so that air can circulate around them to prevent rotting, and then hang them upside down. Taking as many leaves as you can off the stem speeds the drying process. If you're only doing a small quantity, use a coathanger. When they're rustly and papery crisp (this varies from plant to plant) they're ready to store. Flowers and leaves for pot-pourri don't need their stalks, so gently strip them off and put the flowers and/or leaves in cardboard boxes in a dark, dry place. Dry delicate flowers such as borage, loose rose petals, and ornamental flower heads for pot-pourri by the flat air-drying method. You can make a drying frame from a rectangle of timber (an old wooden chair-seat is ideal) with muslin tacked across it. Alternatively just lay your plant material in a dry, warm, dimly lit spot on brown paper, and hope for the best.

Keep herbs for use in culinary, domestic, or cosmetic recipes in airtight jars in cool, dark cupboards. Similarly, the essential oils that often accompany them in recipes are concentrated plant

HANG YOUR CAREFULLY GATHERED BUNCHES OF HERBS IN A WARM, DRY, AND DIMLY LIT SPOT WITH GOOD VENTILATION.

YOU CAN OBTAIN SOFT BLUES, FAWN PINKS AND GREENS FROM MOST EUCALYPT SPECIES – THESE ARE OFTEN INDELIBLE WITH-OUT A MORDANT. THE MOUNTAIN PEOPLE OF NORTH CAROLINA USED TO DYE CLOTHES YELLOW WITH COFFEE DREGS AND TEA LEAVES, USING VINEGAR AS A COLOUR-FASTNESS FIXING AGENT. THE BERRIES OF THE INK BUSH (*PHYTOLACCA*) PRODUCE A RICH BLUISH PURPLE, AS DOES THE ELDER-BERRY. OAK BARK AND ACORNS, AS WELL AS WALNUTS, PRODUCE A BROWN COLOUR. BRACKEN SHOOTS DYE FABRIC LIGHT GREEN AND THE WHOLE OF THE DANDELION, ROOTS AND ALL, CREATE SHELL PINK.

extracts, and should be kept in dark glass bottles so that heat and light don't deteriorate them. Always make sure that your containers are well-labelled with the herbs' date of harvest. (See also pp. 20-2.)

DYEING WITH HERBS

The subtle shades achieved by dyeing fabrics with vegetables and plants *without* a chemical mordant to control their colour seems wonderfully romantic and subtle to the eye accustomed to facto-ry-dyed fabric. It's true that you don't always know quite how pale or dark the result will be, but your pinks will be pearly and lustrous, your blues tinged with a magical violet. It's also true that metallic fixatives such as alum and chrome in conjunction with herbs can give results that vie with synthetic dyes for bril-liance and longevity. But the mordanting process is complicated and long-winded for those who only want to experiment with small articles, and the lovely herbal aromas are masked by the metallic mordant. Non-mordanted natural dyes gradually fade and change, but therein lies their attraction.

Always use absolutely fresh plant material. Firstly wash the plants, then simmer them in a muslin bag (or old stocking) in a large enamel saucepan – about 100 grammes (3 ½ oz) of plant material per 5 litres (2 gallons) of water should do. Don't over-heat it, or you may dull the resultant colour. The item you want to dye must be made of natural fibres – either cotton or wool. Put it in the pan with the bag until it is the colour you are aim-ing for. Some people leave it in the dye overnight to achieve a rich intensity (the fabric will lighten as it dries). Afterwards rinse it in hot, then cold, water before hanging it up to dry in a warm, shady place. (See also pp.20-2 for plant-growing instructions.)

CANDLE-MAKING

You can use plastic cartons or small tins as moulds, or you can dip a wick repeatedly in melted wax to make a candle. Buy wicks from craft suppliers, or make them from string or plaited cotton. Save your old candle-stubs and melt the wax together in a double-boiler or a pan sitting over hot water, first removing the wicks for recycling. Then add a few drops of the essential oil of your choice and some finely chopped herbs or flowers – rose and lavender, rosemary, and mint are favourites, then stir for about ten minutes. You can colour this aromatic mix with children's wax crayons – experiment! If you only have short, recycled wicks, use empty nightlight containers for your candles. (See also p.48.)

To make a larger candle, put a pristine new wick in the centre of a recycled household container of your choice (lightly primed with vegetable oil to make unmoulding easier). Keep the wick in place by tying the top end to a kebab-stick or pencil and pulling the other end taut through a tiny hole in the bottom of the mould, stabilizing the bottom end with sticky-tape. Pour in the melted wax and leave it in a cool place to set. To remove the mould – just warm the outside a little and ease out your candle. Trim the wick and illuminate!

"I will make my kitchen,
and you shall keep your room,
Where white flows the river
and bright blows the broom…"
SONGS OF TRAVEL, 1896

The DINING ROOM

The idea of the "dining hall" came into being in late medieval and early Tudor times when knights, abbots, and other personages of rank felt that they had to display their wealth and power by throwing enormous banquets. The host, his family, and special visitors always sat at a grand "high table", which was literally on a dais, more lowly persons sitting symbolically "below the salt" cellar, on benches pulled up to rough trestle tables. Usually the only other piece of furniture in the room was a cupboard, literally a board for keeping cups on, as plates, or "trenchers", were often at that time just huge hunks of bread devoured with the meat juices at the end of the meal.

Pungent herbs and rushes were strewed on the floor from earliest times – Elizabeth I was partial to meadowsweet, Cardinal Wolsey preferred a scattering of saffron, and the Pilgrim Fathers took with them to America hyssop seeds to grow their favourite floor-covering. Thomas Tusser's *Five Hundred Pointes of Good Husbandrie*, printed in 1573, lists 21 strewing herbs, from violets to "camomill". Eventually, when the smell from the rushes intermingled with food detritus became too offensive they were thrown away to be replaced with fresh, and the floor was usually cleaned and scoured with lavender and rosemary. At the same time the cupboards,

POLISHED, SCOOPED OUT BIG
APPLES MAKE NOVEL CANDLE-
HOLDERS, AS DO CORED
PINEAPPLES.

IT USED TO BE SAID THAT IF A
FLAME BURNED BLUE THERE
WAS AN OTHER-WORLDLY
SPIRIT IN THE ROOM.

(Previous page)
*"That all-softening
overpowering knell,
the tocsin of the soul, –
the dinner bell."*
DON JUAN, LORD BYRON

tables, and chairs were polished with the leaves of marjoram, myrtle, and lemon balm, which imparted shine and sweet fragrance.

You probably don't possess a vast dining-room boasting heraldic carvings, panelled oak, complete with minstrels' gallery, but there is no reason why your dining room shouldn't be as atmospheric a gathering point for family and friends as some of the majestic halls of bygone times. Flickering candlelight automatically lends a mystical, time-dissolving, touch to any dining occasion. The lore attached to candles is varied and vivid. For example, in France and Germany it used to be thought that only a virginal girl could blow life into a dying candle; potentially a source of great social embarrassment for any young ladies present at the dinner table.

> *"How far that little candle
> throws his beams!
> So shines a good deed in a naughty world."*
>
> THE MERCHANT OF VENICE, WILLIAM SHAKESPEARE

There is an equally enormous canon of belief attached to salt, traditionally the salt-cellar must be the first item laid on the table after the cloth, and the last thing to be removed. It seems very easy to offend the Fates in the dining room – to stir another's cup is to invite strife into the home, to put your chair against the wall instead of up at the table when you leave is to invite catastrophe, and to fold your table-napkin after a meal is a certain sign that you will never return to the house. In Britain women should be careful about letting a man pour them a pot of tea or coffee. The sexual symbolism of the spout is apparently an omen for impending pregnancy.

In medieval Europe even noblepersons did not "lay" the table as we know it: everyone brought his or her own knife, spoon, and hard leather cup to the meal and waited with bated breath while the cavalcade of often bizarre culinary displays was fanfared in.

By Georgian times in England forks had made an appearance at dining tables, and table-cloths were thinner because they no longer had to protect the diners' legs from draughts as they had had to do in the barn-like rooms of the 1600s. Huge, showy napkins were much employed, and in upper class England and America the dishes at each course were so numerous that rich hostesses had to draw intricate "maps" of their dinner tables so that the servants would know exactly where to place each one. Sideboards to store the dinner-ware and to serve the food from were *de rigueur* on both sides of the Atlantic, but colonial domestic writer Harriet Beecher Stowe advised that in New England their legs be stood in bowls of water to foil marauding ants.

In modern times yesteryear's bewildering array of dinner-party accoutrements, from compotiers for stewed fruit to chamber-pots in the sideboard for the desperate guest, have vanished. Our preference is not for the finicky doilies and between-courses crumb-brushing of the Victorians, nor for the casually twee hostess-trolley of the 1960s. The dining-room of the green householder harks back to the past in its traditional wooden table and chairs – be they minimalist Shaker Church Family Dwelling style or Gothic Revival, as well as its fresh, relaxing scent of herbal pot-pourri, natural polishes, and mood-setting table decorations made up of fresh spring posies or richly coloured autumn leaf circlets.

But New Age creativity and ingenuity are called for as well. You can do your bit for recycling and be original by using lovely mis-matched old china from second-hand sales. If we look at every-day objects objectively they can usually be employed in different ways. A metal cheese-grater can metamorphose into an impromptu filigree candle-shade, for example, and large, flat shells be used at table as condiment containers. The dining-room can be turned into an interesting and healthy indoor greenspace with bowls and baskets of humidity-promoting, pol-lutant-absorbing plants on the windowsill and around the room. By absorbing negative ions, plants also promote a sense of tranquility and well-being.

"Queen Elizabeth her potion for Wind. Take ginger, cinnamon, galingale, of each one ounce; aniseeds, caraway seeds, fennel seeds, of each half an ounce; mace and nutmegs two drams each; pound all this together and add one pound of white sugar. Use this powder after or before meat at any time. It comforteth the stom-ach, helpeth digestion, and expels wind greatly."
FAIRFAX HOUSEHOLD BOOK,
17TH/18TH CENTURY

SCRATCHES ON THE TABLE
CAN BE STAINED BY
VIGOROUS RUBBING WITH
THE KERNEL OF A BRAZIL OR
WALNUT, BEFORE POLISHING.

*"The several chairs of
order look you scour
With juice of balm and
every precious flower."*
MISTRESS ANN PAGE, THE
MERRY WIVES OF WINDSOR,
WILLIAM SHAKESPEARE

You don't have to be wealthy to decorate your sideboard with a veritable harvest festival of colourful platters of wholesome vegetables and fruit. These can come from your window box or garden, the hedgerows, or your favourite local market; country culinary delights are there for the asking for anyone who is aware of the seasons and enjoys their bounty, provided they use them responsibly, of course.

THE TABLE

This is the most important piece of furniture in the room, an ageless international symbol of conviviality and nourishment. It and its companion chairs (see quote left) deserve a rich home-made polish with a lingering, subtle perfume and a "Shakespearean Housekeeping" history:

THE MERRY WIVES OF WINDSOR BALM

170G (6OZ) UNREFINED BEESWAX
28G (1OZ) PURE GRATED SOAP
½ LITRE (24FL OZ) GENUINE TURPENTINE
½ LITRE (16FL OZ) STRONG LEMON BALM INFUSION
5 DROPS ESSENTIAL OIL OF MARJORAM

Warm the beeswax and turpentine carefully over a flameless heat, as turps is highly inflammable. The double-boiler/bain-marie method works best. Bring the lemon-balm infusion to the boil in another pan, then stir in the soap. When both are cool, mix together until a creamy consistency, then add the essential oil and balm before pouring into a wide-mouthed bottle, or a tin.

Every polished dining table occasionally has to endure **white rings** caused by heat, water, or wine spills. One tried and true method of removing such marks is to sprinkle with a little salt and then rub with a soft rag moistened with olive or linseed oil followed by a polish with a dry cloth. An appropriately coloured child's crayon makes a temporary disguise. You can remove **candle-wax** from polished tables by covering the wax with brown paper and pressing a lukewarm iron on to it briefly.

(Facing page)
*"One cannot think well,
love well, sleep well, if
one has not dined well."*
A ROOM OF ONE'S OWN,
VIRGINIA WOOLF

FISHY SMELLS ARE NOTORIOUSLY LINGERING ON CUTLERY. ALWAYS RUB FISH KNIVES AND FORKS WITH A LEMON TO BE SURE OF EFFICIENT TAINT REMOVAL.

CLEAN GLASS DECANTERS BY FILLING THEM WITH WARM SOAPY WATER, A CUP OF VINEGAR, AND A TABLESPOON OF SALT, OR A SIMILAR AMOUNT OF CRUSHED EGGSHELL.

CANDLES

Fitting candles into candlesticks can be a very trying process, but not if you dip the end of the candle into boiling water first. If you would like your candles to burn down slowly, keep them in the freezer for an hour or two before you want to use them – similarly, popping whole candlesticks in the freezer makes them easy to clean as the wax accretions just snap off. Alternatively, clean them by plunging them in hot water – this is very good if the candle-stubs are stuck fast. Guttering, dripping candles can be prevented by rubbing a little salt around the wicks before you light them. You can make a spectacular yet economical lighting setting with a mass of tiny night-light candles clustered together in a dish of water with different-coloured marbles in the bottom to reflect the light. (See also pp.40-1.)

CLEANING CUTLERY

If your treasured **silver cutlery**, **salt cellars**, and the like become tarnished, it is worth knowing that a quick dip in water in which the potatoes have been cooked will remove the staining. Heirlooms that you use only occasionally should be wrapped in plastic bags and kept in a dark cupboard to keep the tarnish at bay (this rule also applies to silver plate). Rubbing with a little olive oil on a regular basis is also a good anti-tarnish measure, as is milk in the rinsing water.

Silver teapots used on a regular basis should be stored with the lid open and a lump of sugar inside to prevent an unpalatable musty smell developing. A sprinkle of powder starch in the cutlery drawer will keep "everyday" silver bright. **Egg stains** are notoriously difficult to remove from silver – but they come off easily if you rub them with salt on a damp cloth or with a very soft child's toothbrush if there are ornate mouldings. This is also good practice for cleaning fork tines.

Antique cutlery often has bone handles, but you should never immerse these in hot washing-up water or put them in a dishwasher as they will yellow alarmingly and possibly eventually even come loose from the metal part. In addition, silver plate may start to wear off. Instead dip the cutlery quickly in lukewarm, soapy, water and then wipe them dry immediately. The egg on ordinary eggy breakfast spoons just cooks if you put it in the dishwasher and is often difficult to get off with an ordinary hand-wash. If you soak them in the water in which the eggs have been boiled, however, the stains miraculously soak away in a trice.

GLASSWARE

An old butler's hint for achieving really gleaming glassware was to wash the glasses with hot soapy water and then rinse them with cold salt water. Let them drain upside down on a tea towel until dry, and then rub them with a soft linen cloth or washleather. Do not store them upside down in a cupboard or they will harbour a musty smell. For truly brilliant **crystal** – a few drops of ammonia in the washing water and vinegar in the rinsing water will do the trick.

Glass decanters become smelly and stained with a chalky deposit if they are not continuously in use. Old English and North American household manuals invariably advise that they be cleaned by filling with a mixture of warm soapy water, vinegar and salt, or crushed eggshell. Shake the mixture well and rinse thoroughly before use. **Jammed stoppers** can usually be removed with a few drips of warmed cooking oil and some judicious taps with a wooden spoon.

THE SCENTED DINING ROOM

It is not practical to strew our dining-room floors with herbs these days, but there are plenty of other ways we can achieve some of the more delightful moods and scents of yesteryear. Ecologically sound natural fibre floorcovering such as **seagrass**, **coir**, **jute**, plant-dyed ethnic **wool rugs**, or woven **rush matting** provide a good grounding for an evocative dinner-party – they have a wholesome smell and do not make you and your guests feel sweaty in summer and cold in winter like many plastic-based synthetic carpets. The latter can also sometimes give a mild but unpleasant shock from static electricity build-up.

"If you are putting silver away for a length of time, it should be well cleaned first and wrapped in tissue paper. It should not, contrary to custom, be wrapped in baize or any woollen fabric for storing, as wool contains sulphur which will cause tarnish."

THE BOOK OF HINTS
AND WRINKLES

(Overleaf)
FOR A SPECIAL OCCASION
DRAPE THE ROOM WITH THAT ANCIENT SYMBOL OF HOSPITALITY THE GREEN HOP, FESTOONED WITH YOUR FAVOURITE DECORATIONS. SEASONAL VEGETABLES CAN DOUBLE AS BOWLS. WHY NOT SERVE YOUR SOUP IN A HOLLOWED-OUT PUMPKIN?

HOP-HAPPY POT-POURRI

1 CUP EACH OF HEAVILY
SCENTED DRIED ROSEBUDS
OR PETALS, DRIED ROSEMARY,
DRIED HOPS,
CHAMOMILE FLOWERS
½ TBSP DILL SEED
2 CUPS LAVENDER
3 DROPS ESSENTIAL OIL OF
LAVENDER
2 DROPS ESSENTIAL OIL
OF ROSEMARY
1 TBSP OF ORRIS ROOT

Add the essential oils last.
Place in a tightly sealed jar,
or basin, and leave in a warm,
dark, dry place for about a
month, shaking occasionally.
If you are having a romantic
dinner *à deux*, substitute
honeysuckle, also known as
"loves-bind", for the
chamomile.

Dried lavender stems (with heads) stuck in a pot of sand can be used as impromptu incense sticks to scent a frowsty room or remove stale food odours. A plant-mister half-filled with water and about six drops of essential oil of lavender, lemon, or rosemary is a good emergency standby, as is a pan of boiling water with a couple of teaspoons of ground cinnamon or cloves.

It is especially important to have in this room a **pot-pourri** whose ingredients exude relaxation and bonhomie to put new acquaintances at their ease. However it should not be so strong that its scent overwhelms the delicious aromas of your cooking. Hops, native across much of Europe and North America, contain as well as aromatic oils and resins a substance called lupulin, a mild sedative used by some native American peoples as an appetite stimulant. Don't overdo the hops in this earthy combination (see left) or their soporific effect will have your honoured guests snoring into their soup.

There are many imaginative ways in which herbs and flowers can be used at the dinner table. Many are edible, and can be used for flavour and beauty in champagnes, jams, liqueurs, punches, and salads. Their decorative aspect tends, however, to be underused in the Western world. Using crystallized fresh flowers on cakes and chocolates is a delicate Elizabethan art currently enjoying a miniscule revival. Far less challenging, but equally delightful, are homely little touches such as scenting the coffee sugar with a vanilla pod and lavender.

NAPERY

Thank goodness the days have now gone when individual table-napkins could be almost as big as the tablecloth. One welcome past habit, however, is storing the table-napkins with some "sweete bagges" (see p.108), so that they release a lovely scent when unfurled. You can make novel seasonal napkin holders (see facing page) simply by tying them with chunky old-fashioned raffia and incorporating ears of wheat, a holed shell, or clusters of vivid hedgerow berries. Some supple-stemmed culinary herbs – such as chives – can themselves be used as napkin-ties.

TABLE CENTREPIECES

Anything in the centre of the table should be lower than eye-level so that it doesn't obstruct guests' eye-contact and therefore conversation. But flowers are not the only solution and vegetables such as ornamental purple cabbages and runner-bean vines can look most dramatic mixed with flowers. Alternatively you can put a tiny posy in an egg-cup beside each place-setting.

CONDIMENT CARE

Clotted damp lumps in the **salt shaker** were always avoided in days gone by with the inclusion of three or four grains of uncooked rice, an uncooked bean, or a tiny amount of cornflour. Ground pepper invariably loses its pungency and aroma after a while. Always store a couple of whole peppercorns in the container to foil this problem.

STAIN REMOVAL

In the course of family life and jolly entertaining food and drink often makes contact with the floor. **Red wine** on rugs and carpets enjoys a huge stain-removal mystique. Some people say that it comes off best with a soak of white wine, others with soda water, others with salt. Personally I blot it, then use half white vinegar and half warm water with a dash of plain grated soap. **Coffee stains** often respond well to hot water in which borax has been dissolved (a tablespoon to half a litre/16fl oz), or pure glycerine and then a rub with slightly soapy water. The rule with all carpet stain-removal is to avoid saturating it, whatever it's made of. Flattened carpet pile can be made springy again with the edge of a small coin. Dining room carpets and rugs that have become dingy with untreated stains can be rejuvenated with a paste of fuller's earth and a little boiling water, left to dry for 24 hours and then removed with a stiff brush.

MRS BEETON ADVISED
THAT POSIES SHOULD BE
TIED TO NAPKINS
WHENEVER POSSIBLE.

IN ANCIENT ROME,
WEARING A GARLAND OF
VIOLETS WAS SAID TO DISPEL
THE ODOURS OF WINE AND
ALLAY INEBRIATION.

"At meat her manners were well taught withal;
No morsel from her lips did fall,"
THE NUN'S TALE, GEOFFREY CHAUCER, 1392

The SITTING ROOM

> *"But hark! My pulse, like a soft drum*
> *Beats my approach, tells thee I come;*
> *And, slow howe'er my marches be,*
> *I shall at last sit down by thee."*
>
> AN EXEQUY, HENRY KING, 1657

In Harriet Beecher Stowe's Victorian Boston classic *Oldtown Folks*, Uncle Bill admonishes Aunt Lois with "you know nobody wants to go into that terrible best room of yours". We immediately empathize; it makes visitors feel very awkward to be ushered into a sitting room that looks and smells like a pristine parlour or a waiting room at the dentist's. The main family living space and socializing area is perhaps the most important room in the house – this household nucleus should be a versatile, hospitable room: cool and airy in summer and warm and cosy in winter.

In most cultures since time immemorial the hearth has been the home's symbolic focal point. In Celtic and Roman Britain it had not only practical usage but was also the altar of the respective fire-gods Ing and Vesta. Many old houses in Britain still possess vast fireplaces with "inglenook" seats in the corner by the grate. At the height of witch-terror in the 17th century, the lintel over the hearth was supported by a "witch-post", on which was carved the protective X-symbol of Ing. From an environmental point of view an open fire is a pollutant, and, unless contained within an energy-efficient cast-iron stove, a wasteful heat-source. Nevertheless, the age-old, all-age sensory pleasure of sitting staring dreamily at the "pictures" in the flames and smelling the piquantly pungent burning wood is a unique "time-travel" ritual we all like to indulge in on a cold, dark night. In our urbanized, overexplained convenience culture lighting a fire is a welcome primitive pleasure.

The red, glowing "heart", of the home, today's venue for nostalgic multi-generational "homestead-style" wine-mullings and chestnut-roastings, could be a dirty and dangerous foe to our ancestors. The abiding idealized image – granny in her rocking chair with workbasket, grandpa in his snug corner with toasting fork, the dog on the rag-rug, and festoons of corn, herbs, and red peppers drying on the mantel, did indeed exist.

But in the days when the fireplace was also the cookstove accidents were always waiting to happen – splashed lye from soap-making, boiling soupwater dripped from the Dutch oven, long skirts drifting into the hot cinders. No wonder then that people had so many taboos and superstitions centred on the fireplace. China Staffordshire dogs on the mantel and iron fire-dogs both had the same guardianship job, and an adder's skin tacked up the chimney and branches of dried seaweed pinned on to the fireplace beam were common amulets that protected the house from burning down.

Prognostications from cinder shapes were legion – some signified coffins, others cradles – and blue flames always meant a ghost was in the room. The etiquette governing who was allowed to rake the coals was extremely strict. A friend of the family had to wait seven years before he or she could touch the fire-irons: sacred hearth-tending implements were the first thing handed to a bride as she entered her home for the first time. Until early this century in rural areas of Europe and Scandinavia ceremonial "need-fire" was carried to each house hearth from the Beltane or Midsummer bonfire, and was kept going all year by covering the embers last thing at night with a heap of ashes or a domed cover, called in France the *couvre-feu*.

By late Georgian and early Victorian times in middle-class homes fireplaces were smaller, the chimneys shut off during the

IN THE 14TH CENTURY CHARLES VI OF FRANCE ALWAYS INSISTED ON HAVING ANY CUSHIONS THAT WOULD TOUCH HIS PERSON STUFFED WITH LAVENDER.

SAVE GRAND FABRIC SCRAPS AND OLD BROCADE RIBBON AND SEW THEM INTO A POSH PATCHWORK CUSHION. THIS BECOMES ALL THE MORE SPECIAL WHEN STUFFED FULL OF DRIED HEADS OF LAVENDER.

(Previous page)
"Are you sitting comfortably? Then I'll begin."
LISTEN WITH MOTHER,
JULIA LANG

day with ornamental register plates or damper boards. Dirt and how to remove it skilfully, especially from "the best room", became an obsession on both sides of the Atlantic and Australia, too. Drug-store almanacs and how-to-do-absolutely-everything manuals proliferated – from Mrs Beeton's *Book of Household Management*, to Mrs Child's *The American Frugal Housewife.*

Outback Australian and hill-country American wives learned how to overcome their distance from shops by making curtains out of bleached calico flour bags. Calico and fine muslin are in fact a natural, thrifty summer curtaining material for today. For winter many second-hand shops in England have piles of huge old velvet curtains discarded by institutions, schools, and stately homes. They may be a bit faded and grubby – but a gentle wash and a bit of discreet needle and thread and they can look very grand again either at the window (cheaper and healthier than double-glazing) or as draught-excluding *portières* (see also p.26). If you find a pile of old curtains in lovely colours, textures, and patterns that are too far gone to be saved individually you can always cut and create an individual patchwork effect – contrasting indigo taffeta with rough yellow cotton in an interesting way, for example. Specially made tie-backs tend to be expensive – improvise with the easy elegance of contrasting skeins of vivid embroidery silks or tapestry wools.

Attractive, functional storage solutions can be found very cheaply if we adopt granny's resourcefulness. Wooden fruit and vegetable crates from the market make street-chic, cheap stacking systems for everyone's clutter. Rows of simple seagrass shopping baskets on a shelf can similarly hide homework or hatmaking in an instant.

You can conjure illusions of space and a mood of tranquility by using different-sized mirrors with abandon. In interesting old picture frames or home-made ones of, say, weathered driftwood, they almost seem like windows on to another dimension. The Chinese design principle, Feng Shui, holds that reflective surfaces encourage harmony – and if they give visitors a double

"There are families who condemn themselves to perpetual twilight by living in the dimness of closed shutters, to the great injury of their eyes. All this is endured to retard a while the fading of furniture too showy for comfort."

THE BEHAVIOUR BOOK,
MISS LESLIE,
PHILADELPHIA, 1856

FOR MANY CENTURIES
FRENCH HOUSEWIVES
SUCCESSFULLY TREATED
WOODWORM WITH A PASTE
MADE FROM CRUSHED
HORSE-CHESTNUTS.

(Facing page)
THE RED, GLOWING
"HEART" OF THE HOME,
TODAY'S VENUE
FOR NOSTALGIC
MULTI-GENERATIONAL
TRADITIONAL TEA PARTIES
WITH TOASTED MUFFINS,
WINE-MULLINGS, AND
CHESTNUT-ROASTINGS.

helping of your flowers and special *objets trouvés* they will succeed in doing just that.

The patina of age on unpretentious furniture, combined with character paintings and craftwork, good conversation, and the sorcery of the mysteriously alluring scents from your own treatments and polishes should make this a memorable room of laid-back charm for those invited to enjoy the pleasures of your hearth.

THE SCENTED ROOM

Whether or not you are living in a rustic idyll, in this relaxing room you can express your delight in the contrasting textures of natural elements. Here, smooth beach pebbles in a bowl, there interestingly shaped branches and drifts of evocatively faded dried flowers in a junk-shop jug. In the background, your trademark, a subtle old-world perfume.

Since ancient times well-to-do households in Europe and the East scented their rooms with fragrant pastilles made of resins, spices, and herbs heated near the fire in a chafing dish. In modern times people have resorted to a harsh combination of synthetic spray-on "fresheners" and cleansing agents. It is easier to scent the room with simple wreaths of thyme and rosemary and decorative bowls of pot-pourri.

PRESERVING FLOWERS

Sand has been used for centuries as a dessicant with which to dry and preserve flowers. You must remove almost all the stem for this to work. Use silver sand, which is available from garden centres and some pet shops. Dry it in the sun or a low oven, put it in a shallow cardboard box and lay your flowers in it, face up. Fill the flowers with sand and then gently and slowly pour sand all around them as support, and sand over the top of them. You can store them thus in a warm place indefinitely, making sure that when you want to use them (after at least a month) for pot-pourri decoration or arrangements (you will have to carefully push a florist's stub wire through the flower stems for the latter), you remove the crispy flowers slowly and remove the excess sand

IN THE SUMMER, MAKE YOUR
EMPTY FIRE-BASKET BEAUTI-
FUL BY HEAPING IT HIGH
WITH FIR-CONES, LARGE
SHELLS, OR AN EXTRAVAGANT
ARRANGEMENT OF DRIED
FLOWERS.

with a fine paintbrush. Tough, large blooms such as fleshy roses
and peonies dry quite well as they are, hung upside down individually in a dry, dark, airy spot.

SPICE-POURRI À LA MADAME VERNAL

*Keep this mixture in a lidded jar by day. In the evening put
it near the fire with the top removed.*

2 CUPS LAVENDER FLOWERS

3 CUPS DRIED WHITE OR PINK CISTUS FLOWERS

1 CUP EAU DE COLOGNE MINT

1 CUP DRIED THYME

DRIED GRATED RIND 1 ORANGE

3 TBSP ORRIS ROOT POWDER

1 TBSP EACH GROUND CINNAMON, MACE, & ALLSPICE

3 DROPS EACH LAVENDER & GERANIUM ESSENTIAL OIL

2 DROPS GALBANUM ESSENTIAL OIL

UPHOLSTERY AND CURTAIN CARE

Most commercial shampoos for upholstery are similar solvents
to those used in dry cleaning and contain environmental conta-
minants. If your sofas and chairs are just full of **dust** and you
don't have a specialist vacuum cleaner attachment, lay damp
cloths over the dusty bits and give them a good thwack with an
old tennis racquet – all the dust will rise up into the cloth.
Warm water, a pinch of salt, and a little vinegar not only
removes many **stains** but rejuvenates faded colours. Similarly the
vegetable acids and starch in bran make it a good **dry-clean**
material. Rub it on with a clean cloth, and then brush it off with
an astonishing amount of ingrained dirt. You can improvise
with a bit of stale loaf, dough-side down. **Animal hair** on upholstery and cushions can be very off-putting to guests and family
alike. Remove them with a slightly damp sponge, or sticky tape
wrapped around your fingers, sticky side outward. But if the
mess is really too ghastly to rectify, cover the whole lot up with
a colourful throw!

Leather chesterfields and similar **sealed leather furniture** need
feeding if they are not to look dull and start to crack. Some

people use mayonnaise, but the tried and true Edwardian recipe combines the white of an egg, a cup of milk, and a cup of water mixed together thoroughly. Apply with a sponge, let it dry, and then polish it with something soft, yet slightly abrasive, such as a baby's hairbrush.

The traditional French way of keeping **moth** out of heavy curtains is to sew little sachets of southernwood or cotton lavender into the hems (see also p.108). The French also apply talcum powder to old **metal curtain rails** to make opening and shutting the curtains a smooth operation. The easiest way to clean **Venetian blinds** is to wear an old pair of fabric gloves, dampened, and run your fingers over the slats. You can give fabric **window blinds** a new lease of life with a rough flannel dipped in flour. If your **window-frame** is spotted with fly-specks, cold tea will lift them.

THE HEARTH

One of the reasons some people give for not using their fireplace is the damp, **sooty smell** that pervades the room the next day. This can, however, be completely eradicated by throwing dried flowers, berries, leaves, or peel into the fire at the end of the evening (see p.64). The high quantities of volatile oils in lavender, citrus fruit peel, and eucalyptus leaves also make them an excellent aromatic **kindling**.

> *"In lighting fires care should be taken to lay the fire properly… cinders and round coals should be placed at the bottom of the grate, then pieces of wood laid hollow, over which should be a few large cinders laid loose. By this arrangement the smoke goes upwards without impediment. The Housemaid should never fail sweeping down the sutt every morning as high as she can reach."*
>
> THE HOUSEKEEPING BOOK OF SUSANNAH WHATMAN,
> MANUSCRIPT OF 1766, PUBLISHED 1956

"Now stir the fire and close the shutters fast, Let fall the curtains, wheel the sofa round …"
THE WINTER EVENING,
WILLIAM COWPER

RATHER THAN DISCARDING YOUR OLD TENNIS RACQUETS, KEEP THEM ON HAND FOR MERCILESSLY BEATING THE DIRT OUT OF RUGS, MATS AND UPHOLSTERY.

(Overleaf)
"Beauty rests on utility."
MOTHER ANN LEE,
FOUNDRESS OF THE SHAKER
MOVEMENT

ERADICATE A DAMP, SOOTY
SMELL BY THROWING DRIED
LAVENDER FLOWERS, JUNIPER
BERRIES, DRIED SAGE LEAVES,
OR DRIED CITRUS PEEL INTO
THE FIRE WHEN IT IS LOW.

For a romantic evening *à deux* by the flickering flames, toss in handfuls of old, tired pot-pourri and enjoy the ensuing delicious-smelling wafts of smoke. Instead of spending a fortune on kindling wood, make your own from old newspaper.

You can buy contraptions that turn waste paper into kindling bricks, but just as effective is to pulp newspaper in a bucket of water, squeeze out the excess water, and then (wearing gloves), crumple the pulp into tight little balls. When dried they burn really well, but don't use paper with coloured illustrations or toxic lead fumes may be given off when it is burned.

> *"They are curled about the edges, they smell well. And when they are casten into the fire they crake wonderfully".*
> WILLIAM TURNER TALKING ABOUT BAY LEAVES
> IN HIS HERBALL, 1568

If you are anxious about causing **chimney fires**, put your dried potato peel into the kindling of the first few fires of the season. The starch in the potatoes coats any **soot residues** left behind by the chimney sweep with a shiny seal, making it difficult for them to catch fire. It is also a good safety tip to keep a box of damp salt near the fireplace, as this instantly extinguishes flames in an emergency.

Many country folk refuse to burn the wood of the elder tree. This is partly out of respect for the tree, which is useful in all its parts, and partly for folk-memory of its past, steeped in myth and magic. The elder was once known as a tree-spirit called the Hylde-Moer, the "elder-mother", who would haunt any unfortunate who burned her as firewood or made furniture out of her. Traditionally one must never burn hazel, either, because of its water-divining properties.

The summer is the season to pay attention to unused **fire-irons** – corroded brass companion sets can be restored to lustrousness with buttermilk once you have rubbed them down with very fine wire wool or equisetum leaves.

> *"If you ever have to dispose of an old lilac, cut it into logs and burn them, and savour a sweetness of smoke. It is a pleasure one cannot repeat very often."*
>
> A HERBAL OF ALL SORTS, GEOFFREY GRIGSON, 1959

If you have a **wood-burning stove**, the discoloration on the glass doors can be removed with vinegar and water. Similarly vinegar or lemon juice salt can eradicate stains on tiled or **marble surrounds**, but in the case of the latter don't leave it on for more than a few minutes as marble is very porous and bleaches easily.

> *"Take some old newspapers and soak them, then tear into small pieces and roll into small balls. Scatter these over the carpet and brush well with a stiff broom at least once each day. This is a splendid way of freshening the colours of a carpet."*
>
> NEWNES HOUSEHOLD ENCYCLOPEDIA, 1931

CLEANING CARPETS AND RUGS

It is heartbreaking if someone tramples **grease** or **oil** into your favourite rug. However, a sprinkling of dry flour will usually absorb the worst excesses. If that does not work make up a thick paste of fuller's earth and leave it on for several hours. You can blow **soot** off the carpet and on to some adjacent newspaper with the aid of a pair of bellows or an airbed pump. If there is a **black mark** left behind, you can banish it with the application of a generous handful of mixed salt and bran, then removed with a very stiff brush. Slight **scorch** marks from fire sparks disappear if you rub them with the cut edge of a raw onion.

After removing any stain, the original **colour** of the carpet can be instantly reclaimed by rubbing the offending dingy part with a cloth soaked in one part vinegar to three parts boiling water.

STREWING SOUTHERNWOOD OR EUCALYPTUS UNDER THE CARPET REPELS CARPET BEETLE AND MOTHS.

In Scandinavia in times gone by, poets used to sit at their desks wearing wreaths of angelica to inspire them to mystic thoughts.

The old way of keeping **dust** down when sweeping a carpet was to sprinkle damp tea-leaves on it first – if you try this make absolutely sure that the tea-leaves are extremely well-rinsed. Better than tea-leaves, indeed better than a vacuum cleaner for small ethnic-style rugs, is to take them outside, hang them over the clothes line and give them a good walloping, wrong side first, with an old-fashioned woven cane carpet-beater or an old tennis racquet. A few minutes' rest, pile-down, in a patch of clean, damp grass spruces the colours no end.

Dirty **straw matting** becomes clean and bright after a gentle rub with lukewarm, salted water with a little washing soda and lemon juice added. Don't over-wet it. This is also the best way to clean unpainted cane furniture. Let it dry in the sun, not in front of the fire.

Curling **carpet edges** are aesthetically irritating, and potentially dangerous. This phenomenon can be prevented by making up a thick starch paste and anointing it carefully along the edge of the carpet. When the paste has dried, put some brown paper on top and iron it flat. Afterwards, remove the starch residue with a nailbrush, which will also bring up the pile again.

Orris root powder is not only a good **carpet deodorant**, it repels carpet beetle and moths as well. The same can be said of a regular sprinkling with lavender oil, or strewing southernwood or eucalyptus under the carpet. If, however, you are inflicted with a serious infestation, you can kill the larvae by using a hot iron over a damp cloth.

Doggy, **musty smells** in the sitting room can be instantly dispelled with a plant mister filled with water and about ten drops of your favourite essential oil.

Grubby paintwork and wallpaper
Give them both an instant pick-me up by attacking **paintwork marks** with a cut lemon, and **wallpaper scuffs** with a large stale loaf crust, dough-side to the wall. Slice bits off as it gets dirty.

DESKS

Desk **leather** needs special attention. Keep it clean with saddle-soap (sold at good hardware and leatherware shops). You may be able to remove **ink** spilt on the wooden part of the desk by rubbing it with the oxalic acid in a cut slice of ripe tomato.

> *"To write letters of secret that they cannot be read without the directions following:*
> *Take fine Allum, beat it small, and put a reasonable quantity of it into water, then write with the said water. The work cannot be read, but by steeping your paper in fair running water. You may likewise write with vinegar, or the juyce of Lemon or Onion; if you would read the same, you must hold it before the fire."*
>
> THE QUEEN'S CLOSET OPENED,
> THE RECEIPT BOOKS OF QUEEN HENRIETTA MARIA
> TRANSCRIBED BY MR "W.M.", 1655

The purple berries of the pokeweed "Inkberry" were utilized by early American settlers to make ink. In England, decoctions of sloes, elderberries, mulberries, cornflowers, hollyhocks, and fieldpoppy petals were similarly used. Envelopes and parcels were glued with not only sealing wax but the sticky juice of bluebells and mistletoe as well as congealed tapioca.

It is easy to make your own delicately **scented ink** to give your letters a faint but distinctive fragrance (add ten drops of oil of patchouli per small bottle of ink, re-bottle, and label in a romantic fashion). Put lavender oil on a piece of blotting paper or absorbent material, and wrap your notepaper around it. Alternatively store it under a paper bag filled with pot-pourri.

ORNAMENT CARE

Dusting fragile pieces of old **china** can be a nerve-wracking business. Housemaids of long-ago were always instructed to clean antique china and porcelain with a silk handkerchief,

SKIMMED MILK IS AN OLD-FASHIONED BUT EFFECTIVE FIXATIVE FOR PENCIL.

"All locks and hinges and the castors on chairs and sofas should be oiled at least once a year. This prevents rusting and makes them run easily."

THE COUNTRY WOMEN'S
ASSOCIATION OF AUSTRALIA'S
COOKERY BOOK AND
HOUSEHOLD HINTS, 1950

using feathers or a fine sable paintbrush on filigree work. Only use tepid water if washing ornamental antiques. Dust ornate **mouldings** on mirror and **picture frames** regularly with a soft toothbrush. Never clean a **papier mâché** item with soap, but with a sponge dampened with cold water. While still not quite dry sprinkle a little flour over it. Let it stand, wipe off the flour, and polish with a piece of silk.

Copper cache-pots and vases resume their lovely russet sheen after treatment with a thin paste of salt, vinegar, and flour. Leave the mixture on for a few minutes only before burnishing with a very soft cloth. Essential oil of lemon is as efficient as vinegar, and leaves a fresh, citrusy odour into the bargain.

ANTIQUE WOODEN FURNITURE

Woodworm flourishes in damp, humid conditions. A warm, well-ventilated, house should not have woodworm problems. For many centuries French housewives successfully treated the problem with a paste made from crushed horse-chestnuts. However, a regular monthly treatment with the following nourishing, insect-repellent wash, as used in pioneer Australia, is a good safety measure for your heirlooms.

BUSHWHACKER'S BUG BALM

½ LITRE (16FL OZ) BOILED LINSEED OIL
(READY PREPARED)
¼ LITRE (8FL OZ) OF WHITE VINEGAR
¼ LITRE (8FL OZ) REAL TURPENTINE
6 DROPS OF TEA-TREE ESSENTIAL OIL
(THYME IS A GOOD ALTERNATIVE)

Mix well and apply extremely sparingly.
Buff up immediately to a high gloss.

In the 17th century a popular aromatic **polish** for very special furniture was made from beeswax and the crushed seed pods of sweet cicely. American settlers improvised and used the native version, *Ozmorrhiza longistylis*, instead of the *Myrrhis odorata* they were used to in the old country.

PIANOS

Many people do not realize that positioning affects the tone of
the instrument. Its output of volume is improved by placing it
away from the wall. Similarly don't pile books or objects on top
or the tone will be deadened. Sticking **keys** are a sign that your
piano is standing in too damp a spot. You can restore yellowed
piano keys to pristine whiteness by careful wiping with a tiny
piece of silk moistened with lemon juice or colourless alcohol
such as gin or vodka. Don't touch the black keys!

BOOKS

Old books which have **vellum** bindings are great heirlooms. Dip
a soft rag in a little milk and very gently clean the binding, bit
by bit, using a circular motion. Wipe afterwards with a soft,
clean cloth.

Never keep books, especially old ones, above a radiator.
Costmary has been used since medieval times in England and
France both as a strewing herb and to protect books from
insects. In America it is known as the Bible plant, as the flat,
camphor-scented leaves were used as Bible markers by Puritans.
The star-shaped leaf whorls of hay-scented sweet woodruff also
act as an insecticide, and do not mark the page. If you buy some
mildewed books at a garage sale, brush off the mould with a
toothbrush and store the book in a dry, warm place.

"A precious-mouldering
pleasure – 'tis,
To meet an Antique
Book –
In just the Dress his
Century wore
A privilege – I think –"
EMILY DICKINSON, 1862

"Sometimes I sits and thinks,
and then again I just sits."
PUNCH, 1906

The BEDROOM

> *"And still she slept an azure-lidded sleep,*
> *In blanched linen, smooth and lavender".*
>
> THE EVE OF ST. AGNES, KEATS, 1820

The concept of a private place in which to sleep, relax, and recuperate from the stresses and strains of the world is a modern one. Ancient Egyptians, Greeks, and Romans used sophisticated portable wooden beds covered with webbing. Equipped with mosquito netting and hair-do-protecting head-rests, they were minimalist design perfection compared to Dark Age Europe, where people kept themselves off the filthy ground with sacks of dank straw. From Saxon times through to the medieval period people slept where they might, perhaps concealed behind a curtain if they were persons of rank. Even by the self-indulgent times of Louis XIV, the bed might be a gargan-tuan damask-tented affair, but the monarch was expected to entertain visit-ing royals and deal with matters of state in this personal boudoir.

In Eastern Europe, Russia, and Scandinavia people were luckier with privacy, for to deal with the biting winter cold they built their beds in ornate wooden cupboards that became tiny "rooms" when closed. These were often sited in or near the warm kitchen in peasant homes, and are still built by the stove in traditional English vardoes, or gypsy caravans.

In 17th-century England in a well-to-do household the bed was often the most expensive thing in the house – with thick embroidered crewel-work

"Take the flowres and put them in a chest amonge your clothes or among bokes and moughtes shall not hurt them...
Also make thee a box of the wood and smell to it and it shall preserve thy youth."

OF ROSEMARY,

BANCKES HERBAL, 1525

(Previous page)
"Hide me from day's garish eye,
While the bee with honied thigh,
That at her flowery work doth sing,
And the waters mur-muring
And such consort as they keep,
Entice the dewy-feathered Sleep."

IL PENSEROSO, MILTON

curtains and four posts carved with gargoyles and mythic beasts to guard against the terrors of the night. Shakespeare supposedly slighted Ann Hathaway by leaving her only "the second best bed" in his will. Impossibly heavy, treasured beds were transported across the Atlantic by early settlers to the New World – King James sent a four poster with all the trimmings out as a present for Powhatan, the father of Pocahontas. Powhatan had a house specially built for his important bed in the middle of the forest, but never actually visited it. In fact, native American peoples generally preferred springy, aromatic beds made from conifer branches. Similar mattresses were made out of heather by the Scots, moss by the Laplanders, and in France, rustly sweet-chestnut leaves – these noisy beds were known as *lits de parliament*. Until recently the older hill people of North Carolina made mattresses of straw and corn husks, laid on rope webbing. Boston domestic management expert Miss Catherine Beecher would have approved, for one of her favourite maxims was: "there is nothing more debilitating, than to sleep in warm weather, with a featherbed pressing round much of the greater part of the body".

In today's stress-filled society we need our bedrooms to be escapist dream worlds that combine yesterday's natural furnishings and herbal ingenuity with a privacy and peace usually denied our ancestors. Sleep is essential to our good health – after all, this is the place where we spend a third of our lives. Consequently the bed is perhaps the single most important item of furniture in the house. Opt therefore for a natural fibre-filled mattress and pillows instead of sweaty, polyurethane foam. Non-iron polycottons are treated with formaldehyde; it is much healthier to choose crisp untreated cottons and linen topped with woollen blankets, vibrant quilts, and silky, faded old eiderdowns. Electric blankets, it is feared, give off electromagnetic radiation. A hot-water bottle can make even the coldest bed cosy – and old-fashioned nightcaps were not just slumbertime fashion accessories – we lose most of our heat through our heads. The Victorians favoured metal bedsteads instead of the Georgian four-poster because they were fanatical about air-

circulation. However, it is now thought by some experts that a metal-framed, inner-sprung bed near an electro-magnetic field such as a high-voltage power line might act as a conductor for electro-magnetic radiation. If you're not into an eastern sleep-system such as a futon, a wooden bed aligned in a north-south direction in accord with the earth's magnetic field is the answer.

TO MAKE A BED

"1. Air and turn mattress.
2. Tuck in binder tightly.
3. Place undersheet right side up,
broad hem at top.
4. Shake and place bolster and pillows.
5. Place top sheet right side down, leaving
enough at top to fold over.
6. Place blankets and night cover,
tucking in sheets and blankets,
turning top sheet over.
7. Put on bedspread neatly."

DUNDEE HOMECRAFT BOOK, 1937

"And I will make thee
beds of roses,
And a thousand
fragrant posies."
THE PASSIONATE SHEPHERD
TO HIS LOVE,
CHRISTOPHER MARLOWE

The health we are nurturing in our bedrooms is not only physical but mental and spiritual. The importance of the unconscious psyche appearing through the symbolic imagery of dreams was recognized by Carl Jung, who was very interested in superstitions, collective folk memory, and Things That Go Bump in the Night. There are legions of ancient country customs about bedtime, such as that one must "draw close the curtaines to shut out the Moon-light, which is very offensive and hurtfull to the braine". Sound sleep is the answer to Fears of the Dark – King Henry VIII had his own Keeper of the Royal Sleep Pillow to ensure his, and the French writer Colette always had lavender tied to her bedpost to invite the Sandman.

Henry's Royal Sleep Pillow was often cast aside in favour of amorous pursuits. Those feeling similarly inclined should

DAISY FLEABANE WAS USED
BY EARLY AMERICAN
PIONEERS TO KEEP FLEAS
AND OTHER UNWANTED
PESTS AT BAY. IT WAS
STUFFED INTO MATTRESSES,
AND AN OLD PIONEER SUPER-
STITION SAYS THAT IF A
PREGNANT WOMAN TAKES
A FLEABANE SEED FROM HER
MATTRESS AND PLANTS IT
SHE WILL BE ABLE TO TELL
THE SEX OF HER BABY.
PINK-TINGED FLOWERS ON
THE PLANT INDICATE A GIRL,
BLUE A BOY.

perhaps follow the old Indian bridal custom of sprinkling the bed with water scented with erotic oil of sandalwood and the continental one of eating a late-night salad of aphrodisiac nasturtium and basil.

DUST MITES

The average "clean" bedroom houses two million of these microscopic allergen-triggering creatures. They feed on shed scales of human skin, and their pollen-size excretions contribute to the symptoms of asthma and eczema sufferers. This medieval-sounding horror story can be combatted with expensive dust-proof mattress covers and high-powered specialist vacuum cleaners, but there are many sensible low-tech solutions which help.

It helps to ban fixed carpeting, upholstered furniture, heavy curtains, and valances from the bedroom. Avoid using central heating and keep the windows open as much as possible – the mite breeds in warm, humid conditions. Wash your blankets and quilts regularly, or as a desperation extermination measure, put them in a bag in the freezer for half an hour. Grandmother's way of cleaning dust from under the bed and wardrobes was to use a bellows. An airbed-pump does just as well. But if you have serious dust and fluff problems a damp cloth tied over a broom is highly efficient.

TO ALMOST DRY CLEAN A MATTRESS

4 TBS POWDER STARCH

4 CUPS GRATED PURE SOAP

1 CUP FULLER'S EARTH

½ TSP GERMICIDAL EUCALYPTUS OR TEA-TREE OIL

Mix the ingredients and add just enough
warm water to make a paste. Apply thinly and
leave to dry, then brush off vigorously with
a very stiff brush.

In Victorian times it was considered healthy to turn a mattress once a week to even out lumpy filling and shake out any lurking vermin. This is still a good rule to follow.

Bedstead Care

All wooden bedsteads respond well to tender loving care and natural polishes. Rub **oak** with linseed oil for a soft shine, but darker woods benefit from a mixture of two parts linseed and one part natural (not synthetic) turpentine to make them gleam. To keep its lustrous bloom, **mahogany** needs special attention. Wash it down with warm vinegar, warm black tea, or warm beer, dry it with a clean, dry cloth, and then rub it down with a cloth soaked in nourishing linseed oil. Leave the oil on overnight, then wipe off any excess and bring up the wood to a brilliant gloss with a soft, lint-free cloth.

If you have an old-fashioned Victorian **brass** bedstead which has discoloured, transform it with a wedge of lemon dusted with salt. Rub over the brass, wipe off with kitchen towel moistened with vinegar, then polish with a soft cloth until shiny.

Beds must always be placed in the same direction as the floorboards, says European lore. For centuries people have aligned their beds east-west, the path of the sun. There is a universal taboo against having the foot end of a bed toward the door, a superstition having its origins in being "carried out feet-first" following funeral tradition. It is universally thought to be bad luck to get out of bed on the left, or "wrong", side as the left has always had associations with the devil.

Sleep Pillows

The simplest way of promoting tranquility and sleep after a difficult day or an emotional upset is to sprinkle a few drops of essential oil of lavender on a piece of soft muslin and put it inside your pillowcase (not a silk one!) – it doesn't leave a mark. Folk knowledge about the natural soporific qualities of some herbs has been passed down over the centuries since people used to stuff their mattresses with *Galium verum* – lady's bedstraw, and aromatic grasses. The elegant grey or yellow-flowered weed mugwort, a North American and European meadow artemesia, is reputed to produce vivid dreams. Papery hop-flowers are also used in a wonderful old-fashioned tension-beating mixture (see p.77), which

APHRODIZZYSACK

Hang an aphrodisiac bag on the bedpost

MAKE A SMALL DRAWSTRING BAG OUT OF PURPLE SILK OR VELVET. FILL IT WITH FRAGRANT DRIED RED ROSE PETALS AND HONEYSUCKLE INTO WHICH YOU HAVE MIXED THREE DROPS EACH OF PATCHOULI, JASMINE, YLANG-YLANG AND ROSE MAROC ESSENTIAL OIL. TO ENSURE ITS EFFICACY YOU SHOULD STIR THE PETALS WITH A TWIG FROM A HAWTHORN, THE PAGAN LOVE-DIVINATION TREE.

To perfume their hair, banish insomnia and remove "the melancholly", Tudor women of rank slept in quilted caps padded with lavender.

you can sew into a small ornamental cover or slip into the pillowcase stuffing in a large muslin sachet.

The Dressing Table

Always keep your dressing table **mirror** facing away from the window, as too much sunlight will make the silvering cloudy. Clean the mirror with vinegar with a few drops of lavender essential oil in it, there will be a pleasant residual smell and flies will not settle. (See also p.29.)

Hairbrushes can be kept clean and fresh by soaking them every week in two cups of tepid soapy water with half a cup of vinegar or baking soda added. **Combs** can be given a swish round in the same mixture, but don't leave them to soak. To the rinse water add five drops of essential oil of rosemary. Dry in sunlight.

Tiny, tightly packed nosegays of herbs and flowers were carried by Tudor ladies of rank to ward off diseases and horrible smells. By Victorian times these "tussie-mussies" had become love-tokens, and every self-respecting young lady's dressing-table boasted at least one. These charming old-fashioned nosegays make lovely welcome gifts for a guest room. It is traditional to have a large rosebud as the central flower. Surround it with feathery leaves (artemisia is ideal), and bind it tightly with wool. The next layer might be fronds of lavender, hyssop, rosemary, and variegated mint, bound again with wool around the rosebud. The decorative "collar" layer could be alchemilla, ivy, or spotted pulmonaria, tied tightly again with wool (this absorbs water when put in a vase, and keeps the tussie-mussie fresh if the guest wishes to wear it to dinner as a corsage). The whole thing is finished with a trim made out of lace.

In 15th-century Italy undergarments were lavishly sprinkled with fragrant powders. In England pounded cloves and marjoram were kept in Sweete Taffety Bagges for the same purpose.

Wooden **jewellery boxes** were polished and scented in days of old with freshly picked lemon balm leaves rubbed all over the inside as well as the outside of the box. Rub up with a soft cloth. The sheen of **pearls** can be enhanced by periodically rubbing the beads with good olive oil and then polishing them. **Precious stones** in rings, brooches, and necklaces can be cleaned very gently with a soft child's toothbrush dipped in hot water with some soap powder added. To get rid of smears they have traditionally been given a final dip in a colourless alcohol such as gin, but surgical spirit will do.

The same rules apply to **coral** as to pearls, don't wash them since water will rot the thread, and don't let them come into contact with acid, such as vinegar, or they will start to disintegrate. **Glass beads**, contrarily, achieve lustre and brilliance after being polished with vinegar and water. **Jet**, all the rage for Victorian mourning jewellery, is very much back in fashion. Greasy fingerprints on jet have traditionally been removed with a little ball of bread: use the same tip for **amber**. To make amber gleam, wipe it with a cotton bud moistened with soapy water, and then dry immediately, as water clouds its subtle colours. Don't allow perfume to come into direct contact with pearls, amber, and other semi-precious stones, as its alcohol and solvent ingredients will damage them. **Silver** starts to tarnish almost immediately on contact with perfume.

STORING CLOTHES

In the depths of winter, the summer fragrance of insect-repelling lavender issuing forth from closet and chest-of-drawers is a magical treat compared to the acrid pungency of napthalene and paradichlorobenzene crystals.

SIMPLY DIVINE DREAM PILLOW

½ CUP ORRIS ROOT
5 CUPS LAVENDER
FLOWERS
1 CUP DRIED HOP FLOWERS
1 CUP DRIED CHAMOMILE
FLOWERS
2 CUPS LEMON VERBENA
LEAVES
1 CUP ROSEBUDS
½ CUP MUGWORT
FOUR CRUSHED CLOVES

Mix the ingredients together, dusting on the orris root. The pillow should retain its full strength for a year.

ROSEBEADS

In ancient times "Rosaries" were strings of beads made of rose petals, the warmth of the wearer bringing out a ravishing perfume.

3 CUPS DRIED DARK RED ROSE PETALS
2 TSP ROSE ABSOLUTE OR ROSE GERANIUM ESSENTIAL OIL
1 TBSP GROUND ORRIS ROOT
1 TBSP GUM TRAGACANTH
½ CUP ROSEWATER

Grind dry ingredients in a mortar and pestle. Gradually add rosewater, drip by drip, until you have a workable pulp. Fashion little round balls. Pierce holes with a darning needle. Dry on a tray in a dark cupboard for a week. String the beads.

(Overleaf)
"The pleasant land of counterpane."
THE LAND OF COUNTERPANE,
ROBERT LOUIS STEVENSON

You can also stuff lavender heads into handbags, shoes, and gloves put away for storage. If clothes-storing furniture smells musty, the damp and odours can be absorbed by the paper and printer's ink in ordinary newspaper – just crumple some up and leave it in the drawer or bottom of the wardrobe for a few days. When you remove it, sprinkle a couple of drops of delicious-smelling vanilla or clove oil on to cotton wool balls and leave them in its place. Half a dozen sticks of chalk dangling from a ribbon on the clothes' rail will also help get rid of the dank clothes problem.

Many households in North America traditionally use cedarwood chests or cedarwood shavings to protect woollens and vulnerable fabrics against moth and silverfish. You can "cedarize" any wooden chest by rubbing the inside all over with cotton wool soaked in cedar essential oil.

In Australia large eucalyptus gumnuts are an old bush clothes-bug deterrent. The Dutch and the French (and their American colonies) have always favoured southernwood, known as "garde-robe". Gerard's *Herball* of 1633, compiled shortly after the death of Shakespeare, mentions not only the latter herb but also rosemary, tansy, wormwood and thyme as protecting "ye garments from ye moths" and making them "not merrie".

SCENTED DRAWER-LINERS

These luxury items are expensive to buy, but easy to make with left-over wallpaper (some decorating outlets will be happy to let you have their old pattern books for free), and a few drops of the anti-moth essential oil of your choice. Exotic pimento, or "allspice", is invigorating and effective.

Don't put the oil directly on to your ornamental paper, or it will leave a mark – put the oil on to some blotting paper, roll up with another piece of blotting paper and some greaseproof paper, then store your special paper wrapped around the scented parcel for at least six weeks to allow the scent to penetrate properly before using.

IN COLONIAL NEW ENGLAND, TOBACCO WAS USED TO PROTECT STORED FABRICS FROM MOTHS.

MR GERARD'S EXCELLENT GARMENT GUARD
MIX A CUP EACH OF SOUTHERNWOOD, THYME, WORMWOOD AND ROSEMARY LEAVES WITH A CUP EACH OF TANSY AND PYRETHRUM FLOWERS. ADD 1½ CUPS OF SEA SALT, 10 CLOVES AND SEW INTO SMALL SACHETS. PLACE IN CLOTHES' DRAWERS OR ON COAT HANGERS.

SHOE CARE

Smelly shoe problems can be eradicated with a tablespoon of bicarbonate of soda left in each shoe overnight. Emergency **shoe polish** for brown shoes and boots – the inside of a banana skin. If your new **leather** boots or shoes feel a little hard and stiff, leave a couple of peeled, raw potatoes in them overnight and the footwear will be supple in the morning. Grubby **suede** shoes can be rejuvenated by a rub with a vinegary cloth after a going-over with fine sand-paper. Parisiennes have for years kept their **patent-leather** shoes, bags, and belts super-shiny by rubbing them with raw onion and then rubbing off the juice (and smell!) with an absorbent dry cloth till the surface is like a mirror. Olive oil works too. All fine leather shoes and bags like the occasional facelift with raw white of egg left to dry. Take off the residue with a soft rag, then with a clean cloth vigorously buff up a brilliant shine.

" 'The time has come,'
the walrus said,
'to talk of many things:
of shoes –
and ships –
and sealing wax –
of cabbages –
and kings.' "

THROUGH THE
LOOKING GLASS,
LEWIS CARROLL, 1872

MARBEANGROOK BIBBIL (EVENING-STAR EUCALYPT)

An alternative way of scenting the room is with this spicy, sensual pot-pourri recipe from an Australian outback station homestead. As an added bonus, mosquitoes don't seem to like it.

½ CUP ORRIS ROOT

1 CUP EACH ASSORTED DRIED CITRUS PEEL,
DRIED VERVAIN LEAVES,
EUCALYPTUS LEAVES, AGRIMONY LEAVES

4 CINNAMON QUILLS

½ CUP STAR ANISE

A SPRINKLE OF SANDALWOOD RASPINGS

A FEW DROPS OF BERGAMOT ESSENTIAL OIL

"I long to be in a house where the sheets smell of lavender."

ISAAK WALTON

The NURSERY

"Its eyes are blue and bright,
Its cheeks like rose;
Its simple robes unite
Whitest of calicoes
With lawn and satin bows."

THE CHRISTENING, THOMAS HARDY

One of the first things people usually do when a baby is imminent is refurbish a room for a new role as a nursery. The purchasing, painting, and papering is part of the anticipatory pleasure; but it should be borne in mind that some of the room's decorations and furnishings could contain toxins harmful to a tiny infant. More appealing and reassuring by far are simple products with "known" ingredients – such as the myriad bright, clear tints of organic pigment paint; wooden floors enhanced by linseed oil and cheerful cotton rag rugs; unbleached or naturally dyed cotton, linen or wool gracing the cot and providing texture, shade, and warmth draped at the window.

The nursery is an evocative living space – a nurturing room that will feature in childhood memories. It should be cosy, but not oppressive; stimulating but not so over-decorated that the child has no opportunity to use his or her imagination. Continental-style wooden shutters are perfect for shutting out light and intrusive noise for that important afternoon nap. Flywire at the windows is a sensible choice for anyone living in a low-lying area favoured by mosquitoes, gnats, and midges.

Keeping any child's room clean and tidy is always an uphill battle, as dusting invariably means accidentally displacing the sacred pecking order of a

*"Between the darkness
and the daylight,
When the night is
beginning to lower,
Comes a halt in the day's
occupation,
That is known as the
children's hour."*

LONGFELLOW

(Previous page)
*"Sleep, baby, sleep,
Our cottage vale
is deep:
The little lamb is
on the green,
With woolly fleece
so soft and clean –
Sleep, baby, sleep."*

TRADITIONAL LULLABY

line of dollies, or dislodging the drawbridge on a cardboard fort. However houseproud your intentions, children's "clutter" is important developmental debris and must be respected. For safety, wooden floors must be given the minimum of polish, and be regularly patrolled for splinters and sticking-up nails.

It helps to keep furniture to a minimum (maximizing play-space), and to keep the air sweet and fresh with herbal sleep-pillows, delightfully sniffable herbal clothes sachets, and occasional sprays of diluted relaxing essential oils. This is in the spirit of the medieval notion that scents have a direct bearing on physical and mental health. Gypsy mothers have always put sprigs of rosemary under their children's pillows – today the herb's antiseptic and stimulant qualities are universally recognized.

Because of the slim chance in past centuries of infants surviving the first three years of life, a huge number of protective super-stitions amassed on the subject of their environment and welfare. As far back as Ancient Egyptian times small children wore necklaces of garlic to protect against disease. In Ireland up until the last century children wore necklaces of blue beads to frighten off contagion and the Evil Eye, a practice still continued in India, Nepal, and parts of the Middle East. In England and Wales, fairies could not steal babies and replace them with fairy changelings if they were wearing necklaces fashioned from elder tied with red thread.

Throughout 17th century Europe, babies were wrapped tightly in swaddling bands so that they could not move their arms, legs, or heads. In France they lay immobile in cradles decorated with talismans made of the mystic hawthorn, while in England new-born unchristened babies' cribs were decked with amulets made of rowan crosses and salted crusts to prevent the child from being used in sinister witches' sabbath recipes.

A custom which still lingers from christening lore is the belief that the nails of a new baby must not be cut for the first year, only kept trimmed by the mother biting them. Teething was considered a dangerous time, for milk teeth, like bay hair and nail-clippings, were deemed highly desirable commodities in the witch's arcana. That is why teething rings were traditionally made of protective silver and either red coral or red ribbon – red being the age-old protective colour. Another fashionable Christening gift in the 18th and 19th centuries were "layette cushions", heart-shaped pin-cushions with pins arranged to form a verse such as "Welcome Little Stranger".

If they survived to toddler-hood the children of the 17th and 18th century rich were much cossetted. They had foot-warming stoves in their baby-walkers and wore soft fabric crash-helmets called "puddings" to protect their heads as they careered about. Well-to-do children in Victorian England lived in nursery suites entirely separate from their parents. Despite our romantic images of rocking horses and glowing nursery fires, these were often bleak places where Nanny did not always have the charm of Mary Poppins. Other children had to fit in as best they could with adult life – New England youngsters slept in "trundle-beds" that rolled out from under the adult beds at night. Babies delivered by the pipe-smoking "granny midwives" of Georgia earlier in the 20th century often had cribs made out of a bottom drawer or a tin bathtub, while the fearsome 19th-century horse-back riding midwives of the Australian outback wrapped the off-spring of their poorer clients in sugar-bags.

Rural children of the pre-consumer age invariably had "make-believe" dolls made from found objects. Even today the children of Hopi Indians play with cottonwood "Kachina" dolls representing the rain-bearing spirit, and little African girls make themselves playfriends from heads of maize.

In your child's nursery, a relatively minimalist toy cupboard con-taining well-made, non-synthetic, non-toxic playthings, incorpo-rating "findings" and "makings", encourages self-expression and discourages gross materialism at base camp. An important feature of any nursery today should be the nature-table – feathers, skeleton leaves, flowers, and other purist beauties.

HOW TO PRESERVE CHILDREN

"One large, grassy field, one half-dozen children, three dogs, one long narrow brook (with pebble shores, if possible). Mix children and dogs and turn into a field, stirring constantly. Sprinkle with field flowers. Pour brook over pebbles, cover all with deep blue sky and bake in hot sun. When well browned, they may be removed to bathtub and given a good scrubbing, good wholesome food, a prayer, a kiss and a clean bed."

ANON., FROM AN OLD COLLECTION OF AMERICAN RECIPES

Fear of the dark and dread of the secret inhabitants of wardrobes are major causes of insomnia and nightmares in children. Don't forget that creaking doors are often a cause of night-terrors. Prevent this by rubbing softened soap on the end of a pencil into the hinge, making sure that the lead is rubbed in as well.

SPRINKLE A FEW DROPS OF CALMING LAVENDER OIL ON AN OLD, SOFT PILLOWCASE, AND HAVE BY YOU A SPELL-BOX CONTAINING PHIALS OF DIFFERENT-COLOURED "MAGIC" GLITTER. WITH YOUR CHILD, SPRINKLE IT IN THE MOST FEARED SPOTS, SAYING TOGETHER A SHORT JOLLY SPELL. THE INCONVENIENCE OF VACUUMING UP GLITTER IS MORE THAN REPAID BY THE NIGHTS OF UNBROKEN SLEEP.

SLEEPING BEAUTY'S SLEEP PILLOW

This popular concoction is a great bedtime asset for the over-threes. Stuff the fresh-smelling, soporific mixture (after having let it mature in a dark, dry cupboard for six weeks), in a muslin bag, and then put it in a pretty pillowcase or cushion cover concealed by soft filling.

2 CUPS EACH LAVENDER &
DRIED CHAMOMILE FLOWERS
1 CUP EACH DRIED HOPS, MARJORAM
& SCENTED GERANIUM LEAVES
½ CUP DRIED ORRIS ROOT POWDER
1 TSP CRUSHED CARDAMOM SEEDS
2 DROPS EACH LAVENDER, MARJORAM
& CHAMOMILE ESSENTIAL OIL

THE COT (CRIB)

The most important item of furniture in the room should be made of well-rubbed-down, smooth-edged unpainted wood, and finished with plain unscented beeswax polish or a natural varnish. Leaky nappies (diapers) can mean fairly regular **mattress cleaning**. Make sure yours is washable cotton. If you need to give it a freshening once-over use a washing-up bowl of hot water containing five drops of tea-tree oil and two of laven-der. Scrub the offending patch with a specially designated nail-brush. Rinse lightly and let it dry in sunlight, or, in an emergency, use a hair-dryer. When dry, turn the mattress on to the other side and rotate for each "accident". If baby brings up a little feed, the posset can be cleaned off most fabrics with water in which a little bicarbonate of soda has been dissolved.

For a very new baby who is restless, place a bowl of steaming water with just one drop of essential oil of lavender or chamomile in it on the floor below the foot of the cot (crib) to give the room a calm, clean atmosphere. In the old days whenever a small child was sick, old-fashioned nannies used to spray the room with a germicidal half-water, half-vinegar solution. This is still a good **air-purifier**, but add a couple of drops of antiseptic rosemary essential oil.

In medieval times fretful babies were often soothed with a chamomile **sleep-cap**. This lovely idea – a quilted hat with calm-inducing chamomile flowers stuffed in each section – has a timeless appeal. Instead of the heavy quilting, sew dried chamomile blossoms into the head-band part of a close-weave soft cotton, silk, or satin bonnet for daytime wear only. Make sure there are no uncomfy wispy stem parts sticking through. If you embroider a chamomile flower on the ribbon rosette and the child's name on the headband this makes a unique birth gift.

Children and babies toss and turn so much that their duvets and quilts quickly become lumpy, with the filling usually accumulating at one end. Take a leaf out of the household books of the Swiss, Austrians, and Dutch – on fine days air the duvet by hanging it out of the window, and then beat it with a carpet beater, stick, or old tennis racquet to fluff up the feathers and distribute them evenly. You can make sad, elderly baby blankets soft and fluffy again after a wash by this same violent method when you hang them on the line to dry. Cellular cotton blankets are in fact the healthiest all-weather choice for babies and children, ideally complemented by hundred percent untreated cotton flannelette sheets. Always wash new bed linen before use to get rid of any residual chemicals.

BOTTLES

The old-fashioned, and best, way of preserving the **teats** (nipples) is, immediately after use, to rinse them in cold water and rub inside and out with a sprinkling of sea-salt. After a five-second plunge in boiling water they can be put on a saucer (which has also been sterilized by boiling water) and covered with a clean basin or cup.

KEEP INSECTS AT BAY IN THE NURSERY WITH POTS OF BASIL, LAVENDER, OR LEMON-SCENTED EUCALYPT ON THE WINDOW SILL, OR A LITTLE BUNCH OF LAVENDER TIED TO THE MOBILE OVER THE COT (CRIB).

"And sometimes she has went to places they didn't even have a diaper to put on th' baby, and she'd take old sheets – most of it was linen, you know, they're good and soft – and she'd go and they didn't have diapers, so she'd sit and notch' em instead of hemmin' em. Take her scissors and notch that baby a bunch of little diapers out of what she carry."

MRS ELIZABETH PATTERSON,
TALKING ABOUT HER MOTHER,
ONE OF THE CELEBRATED
"GRANNY-MIDWIVES" OF
GEORGIA. FOXFIRE 2, 1973

NAPPIES (DIAPERS)

Disposable nappies (diapers) are alas, ill-named. Millions are used each day and most of them end up on land-fill sites as their plastic linings are mainly non-biodegradable. Their innards are made of paper pulp bleached in an environmentally unsound process. The towelling version may seem like hard work, but they are more ecologically friendly and a good deal cheaper in the long run! The cleaning process can be quite simple if you use a gauze liner to trap any soiling.

Many commercial nappy (diaper) soak cleaners contain "brightening" irritants which can exacerbate nappy-rash. Use a mild borax solution instead, and then wash them in as hot a wash as possible. Sunlight is the best bacteria-killer and bleaching agent there is, but if there is serious yellowing and the weather is rotten you can brighten them up by soaking them overnight in a bucket with a teaspoon of cream of tartar added to lukewarm water. Beer-making buckets are excellent for soaking because of their large size and extremely tight-fitting lids. Don't dry nappies (diapers) on radiators as they become stiff as a board and chafe against baby's skin.

A bare bottom is the best nappy (diaper) **rash** treatment there is. Some baby creams and lotions contain petrochemicals. Instead, use olive oil on cotton wool; it's more soothing than water. Finish off with a mild herbal cream made with cooling calendula or calming chamomile.

CLOTHES STORAGE

You can give baby clothes a delightful subtle aroma if you store them in a cupboard or chest of drawers among scraps of ribbon which have been scented. You can do this by wrapping them in tissue paper in a bowl of pot-pourri for a couple of weeks. Remember, if you have acquired an old Christening gown, wrap it in blue tissue paper to keep it from yellowing. If the garment is very old, delicate, and special (beaded, heavily embroidered, or made of lace), it should be cleaned and repaired only by a qualified textile conservator and stored in specialist acid-free tissue paper. On no account keep it in a polythene bag, as the static electricity it produces encourages dust, and the trapped moisture is an invitation to mould and mildew.

Once past the toddler stage, children enjoy finding simple shaped lavender sachets made from scraps – dollies, chicks, or teddy bears – among their clothes. The gentle spicy perfume of rosemary, cloves, and rosebuds mixed together is popular with children, and is also a germicide.

Remember when you are **name-tagging** your young children's clothes in preparation for pre-school that they probably cannot yet read! Instead, a specially chosen "identity button" with a favourite animal or flower motif sewn somewhere comfy inside will be very popular and help the child keep track of possessions. Shoes and boots can be marked inside with colour spots to help distinguish left from right. The best way to stop children's **mittens and gloves** getting lost is still the age-old nanny trick of attaching one to each end of a long piece of elastic and threading it through the sleeves of the coat or jacket.

FOOTWEAR CARE

To prevent children bringing sand into the house on a beach holiday, stand them outside and rub talc into their gritty feet and legs. The talc absorbs the moisture in the damp sand and it can be brushed off immediately.

If **leather shoes** become stained by sea-water, get an egg cup of hot water with a pinch of washing-soda added. Rub well into the stains with a toothbrush, allow to dry, and polish. Remove tar from **canvas sandshoes** by scraping off as much as possible, then thoroughly damping the spot with salad oil or melted lard. Leave it for 24 hours to allow the fat to penetrate, then scrub with soapy water and a nailbrush.

Freshen smelly **trainers** when they have become sweaty or damp with a piece of charcoal in a clean old sock or a paper bag. Baking soda works as well. To save time and temper, clip pairs of

TISTY TOSTY "TALC"

This Elizabethan flowery fragrant powder is better for baby's skin than real talcum powder, which is a mineral derivative that can cause allergies in sensitive skin.

2 CUPS CORNFLOUR

1 CUP ARROWROOT POWDER

½ CUP ORRIS ROOT

2 DROPS CHAMOMILE
ESSENTIAL OIL

3 DROPS ROSE GERANIUM
ESSENTIAL OIL

Mix the dry ingredients together, then add the essential oils, drop by drop, stirring. Put the Tisty-Tosty in an old-fashioned talcum-powder drum. Add a couple of grains of rice to prevent damp lumpiness.

(Overleaf)

"As soon as a child has left the room, his strewn toys become affecting."

JOURNALS, EMERSON, 1839

A COUPLE OF SPOONS OF
VINEGAR IN HOT WATER IS
AN EXCELLENT CLEANER
FOR CHILDREN'S
WOODEN TOYS.
RINSE WELL.

shoes together with clothesline pegs, and pop them in a vegetable rack at the bottom of the wardrobe.

To assist toddlers' early-walking equilibrium – lightly sandpaper the bottom of their shoes so they have a better grip on floor surfaces to help them master those first crucial steps.

CLEANING
In children's bedrooms quick dusting is often all there is time for in the hectic round of daily events. Vinegar and tepid water on a wash-leather imparts not only a fine gloss to **woodwork** but also a fresh smell. It's sensible to have a gaily-patterned oil-cloth on the nursery table, but this often becomes very dirty and loses its shine after a few nursery teas and some enthusiastic finger-painting. A half-and-half lotion of turpentine and warm milk is an excellent restorative.

Rejuvenate grimy, fingermark-covered **paintwork** and painted children's **furniture** by rubbing it with a worn loofah before washing it with warm soapy water. If the dirt is very bad indeed add about 56g (2oz) of borax per litre (32fl oz) of water. Rinse and wipe dry.

Cunning parents prevent or disguise **scribble** and **graffiti** by using cardboard egg-boxes or egg-crates as sound-proofing material on the nursery walls. Children enjoy painting them vivid colours with non-toxic, water-based poster-paints, and they are infinitely replaceable. Another nursery wall tip is to stick cheap lining paper all around the room and encourage the children to express their creativity on it – murals, family, and pet portraits, leaf-prints, potato-prints . . . these walls are heaven for those interminable wintry, rainy days.

FLOORS
Washable **wood**, **cork** or **lino** floors are ideal for the heavy-duty traffic of a children's room, but remember if you do have a carpet that a good **underlay** prolongs its life considerably. Hairfelt underlay is the best quality available. Foam-rubber or

composition-backed underlay is petrochemical-based, deteriorates unevenly and causes uneven wear. For thrift, use layers of brown paper as an underlay under a cleaned-up second-hand wool rug. Remember that most synthetic carpets have been treated with fungicide and formaldehyde – not really what you'd want your baby to crawl on.

Remove **scuff marks** and junior artist scribblings on lino with neat eucalyptus oil, and try getting **chewing gum** off carpets (and children's clothes) with a cellulose-based paint-thinner or with an ice cube pressed on the gum until it is frozen and cracks off easily. The latter method sometimes works on children's hair, but usually the scissors have to come into play!

TOYS AND TOY-CARE

Imaginative playthings for children of all ages need not cost a fortune. A trip to a second-hand sale furnishes the dressing-up box. Dolls' houses are just as much loved for being four cardboard boxes glued together as they are for being wooden Georgian mansions. Puppets can be made from gloves; playdough from flour, water, and salt; hobby-horses from a broomstick, a filled sock, some buttons and braid; jewellery from string, paint, and uncooked pasta. Swap non-special toys with friends for a few weeks to broaden the play horizons.

Make sure that if your children use felt-tip marking pens that they don't contain chemical solvents. New-ish felt-tips that appear prematurely dried up can often be given a new lease of life by dipping them in vinegar and storing them upside down.

TEDDY DRY-CLEANING
IF MUCH-CUDDLED BUT SQUALID-LOOKING SOFT TOYS ARE NOT SUITABLE CANDIDATES FOR THE WASHING MACHINE, CLEAN THEM BY SHAKING THEM AROUND IN A BAG CONTAINING BAKING POWDER. THE DIRT AND GREASE SHOULD ADHERE TO THE BAKING POWDER, AND DIZZY TEDDY CAN BE CAREFULLY BRUSHED OFF.

"Star light, star bright,
very first star I have seen tonight,
Wish I may, wish I might,
Have the wish I wish tonight."

TRADITIONAL

The LAUNDRY

"Twas on a Monday morning
When I beheld my darling;
She looked so sweet and charming
In every high degree
Yes! She was so neat and willing O,
A-picking up her linen clothes;
And dashing away with the smoothing iron,
She stole my heart away."

TRADITIONAL

The sumptuous palace of Versailles may have been legendarily filthy, but King Louis XIV always insisted that his shirts and sheets were rinsed in jasmine and musk waters. Alexander the Great preferred myrrh, and Charlemagne was partial to a rose-scented rinse for his raiment. Shah Jehangir Khan, builder of the Taj Mahal, commanded that his jewel-studded suits be stored in cupboards scented with patchouli. Marie Antoinette and Napoleon's Josephine liked their dresses to exude a violet scent as they swished by, while Elizabeth I ignored the newly imported exotic aromatics of the Levant and commanded the royal night- and under-apparel to be washed in lavender water. The rigours of scrubbing, boiling, wringing, and ironing were arcane mysteries to these uppercrust persons.

The aroma of lavender has been associated with cleaning and scenting clothes at least as far back as the Roman times (the word is derived from the Latin, *lavare*, to wash). Whatever the era, until very recently the household wash has been an enormous body of work with many complex rituals and superstitions. The Aboriginal peoples of Arnhem Land in Australia's Northern Territory make full use of all the plants in their tribal areas, making rough all-purpose washing soap out of the leaves of the indigenous red ash tree. In France country people used to make a wool-cleansing soap out

FINISHING OF KNICKERS
"1. Iron trimming and double parts on wrong and right sides.
2. Iron front and back of legs on right side.
3. Air."
DUNDEE HOMECRAFT BOOK

of conkers from the horse-chestnut tree, while in England contemporary museums and historic-house textile conservationists still use the gentle, dirt-absorbent foaming vegetable saponins in saponaria, or soapwort, to clean valuable antique fabrics. The plant is still widely used for domestic purposes in the Middle East. Also known as *herbe à foulon*, or fuller's herb, it has a natural bubbly green leaf-lather, and was brought to England from German and French monasteries by friars and pilgrims. It was planted near textile mills to be used by the fullers (cloth workers), and taken to North America by colonists as an essential practical herb, where it was known as My Lady's Washing Bowl.

As commercially bought soap was taxed in England until 1865, washing soap was usually home-made from hog-fat and lye from wood-ash or fern-ash, sometimes coloured with beetroot or carrot juice and perfumed with herbs. In the Australian bush at the turn of the century women made it out of clarified dripping, rain water, caustic soda, and machinery oil.

Many cleaning techniques from bygone years – the use of lemons as a bleaching agent and the oxalic acid in tomatoes as a stain-remover, for example, are potent, and do no harm to humans, animals, or the environment. Harmful chemicals contained in brand-name washing powders include fluoroscar "brighteners", water-softening, bleach-activating agents that bond with heavy metals and can end up in our drinking water, phosphates which starve aquatic life of oxygen, and bleaches with potentially carcinogenic organo-chlorine by-products.

(Previous page)
"O Mrs Higden, Mrs Higden you was a woman and a mother, and a mangler in a million million."
OUR MUTUAL FRIEND,
CHARLES DICKENS, 1859

The prototype for the automatic washing machine was the nautical practice of towing dirty clothes behind the sailing ship. The first washing machines were cumbersome items, containing great lumps of concrete weighing half the weight of the machine to slow down the vibration in the spin-cycle. Before concrete was universally used, machines had to be bolted to the floor to prevent them "walking". Today's ecologically aware householder does not have to get back to such challenging basics, but can choose an energy-efficient, low-water-usage, hot-fill model. This is a sound option when you consider that the average machine uses 100 litres (22 gallons) of water per cycle; more than twice that of hand-washing.

> ### To Make A Speciall Sweet Water to Perfume Clothes in the Folding being Washed
>
> *"Take a quart of damask water and put it in a glass, put into it a handfull of Lavender flowers, two ounces of Orris, a dram of Muske, the wight of fourpence of amber-greece, as much civet, four droppes of oyle of cloves, stop this close, and set it in the sunne a fortnight; put one spooneful of this water into a bason of common water and put it into a glasse and so sprinkle your cothes therewith in your folding."*
>
> DELIGHTES FOR LADIES, SIR HUGH PLATT, 1594

In the past, laundrywork, especially for heavy homespun linen, was a problematical business requiring great stamina and taking at least a day to complete. Unlike Beatrix Potter's little hedgehog washerwoman, Mrs Tiggywinkle, with her "nice hot singey smell", most housewives had more than Cock Robin's waistcoat and some hankies to contend with. They employed a battery of heavy wooden implements with which to wage war against vast mounds of dirty textiles: the wooden washing block, the ridged battledore, the conical agitator called a washing dolly, and the aggressive-looking washing bat called a beetle. Very soiled articles were boiled at length in a giant fire-heated pot called a copper. In outback Australia, pioneers used hollowed-out eucalyptus logs for the same purpose.

In Europe the brilliant white of sheets on the line was a matter of great pride for country mansion housekeeper and slum tenement resident alike. In Holland and Germany bedlinen was kept white by hanging it out of the window to air and bleach in the sun. English women helped nature along by using the "blue-bag" in the final wash – a sachet of blue powder made from the

HOME-MADE
WASHING POWDER
1 CUP PURE VERY FINELY
GRATED SOAP
1 CUP WASHING SODA
2 TSP LAVENDER OIL

FRIENDLY FABRIC RINSE
1 CUP BICARBONATE OF SODA
1 CUP CIDER/WHITE WINE
VINEGAR
2 CUPS OF WATER
1 TSP LEMON OIL
1 TSP EUCALYPTUS OIL

(Facing page)
"No perfumes, but very fine linen, and plenty of it, and country washing."
MEMOIRS OF
HARRIETTE WILSON, 1825

indigo plant. Before drying the clothes were passed through a mangle – the earliest sort consisted of a box containing a fair quantity of stones.

Drying in crowded towns was often done on communal drying grounds outside the city walls. Everything was spread on the ground to dry, often with dismaying results! In rural regions the drying was often draped on aromatic bushes – a custom followed by Europe's Romany people to this day. Indoor drying was festooned over the solid-fuel stove on a pulley.

Monday was the favoured washday throughout Europe because women felt strong after a day of relative indolence, and usually had something left from Sunday to feed the family with.

Weather forecasting was all important. The significance of clouds, morning dew, and the haziness of the sun and moon – were all serious talking points. In England it was considered bad luck to wash new clothes while the moon was new, and disastrous to do washing on New Year's Day (one of the family might be washed away), or on Good Friday, when legendarily, washerwomen jeered at Christ on his way to Calvary.

Ironing has changed dramatically since Roman times, when togas and cloaks were ironed with large flat stones or specially crafted glass "smoothers". In the 17th century courtiers goffered their enormous ruffs with heated "poking sticks". In the early 19th century there was a huge range of pre-electric irons on the market, from the heavy Austrian box-iron to the tiny Italian tally-iron, all designed for different applications.

Today, the storage of clean linen is as accompanied by ritual as it was in Ancient Egypt, when it was folded away with myrrh and religious amulets. Chests and trunks made of aromatic wood – cedarwood, cypress, and sandalwood being the most popular, are still employed throughout the world. In English linen closets and French armoires, lavender, hay-scented woodruff, and southernwood have been traditionally used to keep fabrics crisp

ROSEMARY IS LEGENDARILY
BELIEVED TO HAVE GAINED
ITS SCENT FROM THE
GARMENTS OF THE INFANT
JESUS WHEN MARY HUNG
THEM TO DRY ON A
ROSEMARY BUSH.

and fresh and vermin at bay. Indian precious saris are scented with insect-repellent patchouli oil and scattered with basil, the sacred herb of Krishna and Vishnu, while broken shards of cassia bark and clove bud oil fragrance Malaysian and Indonesian linen-cupboards with delightful aromas.

STAIN REMOVAL

Avoid the flammable, hazardous substances in proprietary stain-removing solvents and use instead the natural, non-toxic remedies used for centuries past. Remove all stains as quickly as possible. Always work from the outside of a stain inwards, to prevent it spreading. Afterwards wash well, boiling if the material is robust enough. All of the following are for washable fabrics only.

To remove **dry blood** – soak in cold, salted water for 12 hours, then rinse. Remove tiny blood stains with saliva. For silks and satins make a thick paste of starch and water. When the paste is dry, brush off with a soft brush. To remove **wet blood** – use pure soap grated into lukewarm water with a little washing soda.

For **milk stains** rinse with cold water to remove the albumen, then hot to disperse the fat. Wash in soapy water in which a little borax has been dissolved, then rinse. For **egg stains** soak in cold water before washing in hot, soapy water. Eradicate **perspiration stains** using glycerine applied with a nail-brush and left on for an hour before the main wash.

> ### TO MAKE BORAX SOAP
> *"Put together plain soap, borax and hot water in the following proportions – 1lb of the soap cut into small pieces, 1oz of powdered borax and 1qt of hot water. Mix the ingredients together over the fire, but see that it does not boil. When it is cold, cut it into cakes and use it like common hard soap."*
>
> THE YOUNG HOUSEKEEPER'S FRIEND,
> MRS CORNELIUS, BOSTON, 1848

POTATO-FLOUR-WATER FOR
A YOUNG LADY'S DELICATE THINGS

*"A new way of using potatoes as a whitening
agent has been recently proposed. After washing
and scraping them with a brush one puts them
into boiling water until they fall into
little pieces in the way they do if one wants to
make pot-flour. Push them through a sieve. Pour
the mucilaginous liquid off the white pot-flour
precipitate, and keep it for later use. When the
items to be cleaned are spread out on a table,
one rubs them gently but repeatedly with this
liquor. After, wash them well and dry them.
This procedure is proposed for
delicate silk, wool and cotton materials."*

MANUEL DES DEMOISELLES, PAR MADAME CELNART,

PARIS, 1827 (EXCERPT TRANS. B.PAGRAM).

STARCHING WAS FIRST
INTRODUCED TO ENGLAND
BY A FLEMISH HUGUENOT
REFUGEE, DINGHEN VAN
DEN PLASSE, IN THE 16TH
CENTURY. LONDON WOMEN
PAID HER FIVE POUNDS TO
LEARN THE TECHNIQUE.

To eradicate **grass stains**, damp the mark with cold water, apply cream of tartar, and rub lightly with a nail brush before rinsing.

For **fresh tea** and **coffee stains**, pour boiling water over. If dried, soften the stain with a solution of "glycerine" warm water or water with a little borax dissolved in it, leaving the solution on for an hour before rinsing. Rinse **cocoa** or **hot chocolate** first in cold water before applying the above method. For **fruit stains** rinse with cold water. If the stain is fresh, stretch the fabric over a large bowl, sprinkle with salt or cream of tartar and pour boiling water through. Treat dried stains with a glycerine or borax solution, before washing.

For **mildew** rub with buttermilk, then wash in hot soapy water. Or try a paste of equal amounts of starch and salt, dampened with lemon juice. Dry in the sun, if possible. For **wine stains** apply white wine to fresh red wine spots. After a minute or two, rinse with cold water. Dried stains on reasonably robust fabrics come out if dipped in boiling milk. Rinse in cold water.

(Overleaf)
*"5, 6, 7, 8, 9 . . .
Hang your washing
on the line."*
TRADITIONAL SKIPPING
(JUMP) ROPE RHYME

To Freshen A Veil
"Put the veil on the
ironing-board, stretch a
piece of wax paper over
it and press with a
moderately hot iron."
GRANDMOTHER'S
HOUSEHOLD HINTS,
HELEN LYON ADAMSON

For **ink stains** rub fresh stains with a paste of milk and starch, re-applying when it discolours. Leave it on for a couple of days until the milk sours, or alternatively use buttermilk. Salt and lemon juice works better on delicate fabrics. If the stain is old, soak in onion, sorrel, or tomato juice before a hot wash. Country people say urine is also very efficacious! For **iron mould** lemon juice and salt usually does the trick. To get rid of **tar, creosote,** and **gloss paint** scrape the worst off with a blunt implement, then rub with eucalyptus oil.

For **waxes, fats** and **oils** treat greasy marks with a weak washing soda or borax solution. An old French folk remedy which sometimes works is applying the yolk of an egg, leaving for half an hour and then washing with soapy water. If you have spilt gravy on wool or silk, apply a paste of fuller's earth and water, brush off when dry. **Sea-water** leaves unpleasant stains, especially on dark material. Neat white wine vinegar usually works.

WASHING
Most **commercial detergents** contain artificial fragrances, dyes, optical brighteners, enzymes, bleach, petrochemical surfactants, and phosphates. From an environmental and human health point of view this seems like chemical overload. Many of these chemical residues linger on the fabric after the wash and set up allergic reactions in those with sensitive skin. But there is an effective, safe, biodegradable alternative.

If you are using natural fabrics, you don't strictly need conditioner, whose purpose is mainly to diminish the anti-static cling of synthetic materials. A half cup of cider or white wine vinegar added to the soap powder with your usual load acts as a **fabric softener** and **mould inhibitor.** This easy do-it-yourself biodegradable rinse makes clothes soft and smell fresh too. Use it in the same way as you would an ordinary conditioner.

Rejuvenate grey underwear by putting some pieces of freshly cut lemon or orange in a muslin bag in the hand-wash rinse water. The citric acid is a **natural bleaching agent** and water softener –

the fruit also imparts a fresh fragrance. A small piece of orris root in the rinse water will also make them smell delightful.

If you are not sure if you have got all the soap out of your clothes in a hand-wash, put a cup of vinegar in the final rinse. Non-colourfast items should be washed by themselves, and rinsed in salted water. Such a rinse keeps silks soft and vivid. A colander is very useful for getting the water out of delicate small items you do not wish to wring too vigorously.

The gentle saponins in soapwort make it a favourite with textile conservators. Use it on your delicate old fabrics and tapestry cushions. If you don't have any in your garden, the dried root of saponin is obtainable from most herbalists. (See recipe, below.)

Woollens should also always be washed by hand in lukewarm water. Having the water too hot is the major cause of shrinkage, as is rubbing the fibres too vigorously. Rinse well, or soap residues will make the garment look thick and "felted". Soak new woollens in rainwater for a couple of hours. It helps to retain the oil in the wool when one later washes with soap powder. When the woollens eventually become dry and scratchy, a few drops of eucalyptus oil in the rinse water helps replace the depleted natural wool oils. Brush off the annoying **pilling** on old sweaters with a wet nail-brush.

SOAPWORT CONSERVATION CLEANSER
HALF A CUP OF DRIED SOAPWORT ROOT OR A
COUPLE OF HANDFULS OF FRESH STEMS
1 LITRE (32FL OZ) OF WATER

Chop the fresh stems or crush the dried root, having soaked it overnight. Simmer the soapwort in the water in an enamelled pan for about half an hour, giving the occasional stir. When cool, strain and use to gently sponge soiled areas. Rinse well.

Starching clothes has gone somewhat out of fashion. If, however, you need to stiffen and gloss-up some table napery or

HERB BAGS
FRAGRANCE YOUR LINEN
CLOSET BY SCATTERING
LITTLE SACHETS CONTAINING
YOUR PERSONAL SELECTION
OF HERBS SPRINKLED WITH
ESSENTIAL OILS.

collars and cuffs, improvised starch can be made out of water in which rice, potatoes, or pasta has been cooked. Dip in the items and iron them while still damp.

DRYING

Remember that the sun's rays are the best **germicide** and **whitening agent** there is. So, although the habit seems to be dying fast, use the washing line, if you have one, and the brisk refreshing breezes rather than the energy-extravagant tumble dryer. If the weather is inclement, make use of indoor heat by hanging the drying on wooden airers. Or make use of an old-fashioned airer on a pulley in the kitchen. If you are installing one of these sought-after items, a good place to situate it is at the top of a stair well, where all the house's heat accumulates.

Copy the habits of Tudor and Elizabethan gentlewomen – plant a row of lavender and rosemary bushes near the clothesline and use them to dry special underwear, delicate scarves, handker-chiefs, and baby clothes – they will have a delightful fragrance and be moth-repellent, too.

Put a handful of salt in your final rinse-water, it will stop your clothes freezing solid on the line in deep winter. Poor Della Lutes recalls in *The Country Kitchen* how the clothes froze into "rigid effigies" the moment they were hung out to dry. Clothes pegs often leave marks on jumpers. Use, instead, old stockings pulled through the sleeves and tied by the feet to the line. Peg sheets by the edges rather than folding them over the line – they will billow far more effectively. Always dry trousers and jeans inside out so that the bulky seams and pockets are exposed. On a hot summer's day dry all the clothes inside out so they are not faded by sunlight. Dry woollens flat on a thick towel, or care-fully pin them to a heavy sheet on the line.

IRONING

If you discover **starchy deposits** stuck to the bottom of your iron, rub the base with a cut lemon dipped in kitchen salt. Remedy **rusting** with a duster full of crushed candle ends – rub the surface of the just-warm iron over this waxy "pad" and it will run smoothly. If you are unfortunate enough to make iron burn marks on any fabric, make a paste out of white wine vinegar, salt, and pure grated soap, rub it into the marks, and then rinse out with lukewarm water.

Ideally, **velvet** shouldn't be ironed, but hung up in a steamy bathroom so that the creases fall out. However, if it is very crushed, hold a hot steam iron just above the pile to restore it. Iron **woollen material** through a piece of damp muslin to avoid "shiny" patches. Shine can be removed from clothes by sponging the material with a strained, cooled decoction of ivy leaves boiled with a little water. **Silk** should be ironed on the wrong side with the iron on its lowest setting, or on the right side through tissue paper. Iron **embroidery** on the wrong side, with the stitchwork face-down on a thick towel. Use yourself as an emergency **trouser-press**: dampen the desired creases and put the trousers beneath your underblanket when you go to bed at night. Ironing trousers through newspaper gives them a sharp crease.

TO MAKE YOUR BUTTON THREAD REALLY TOUGH AND PREVENT UNNECESSARY BUTTON LOSS, FOLLOW THE OLD TAILOR'S TRICK OF RUBBING IT OVER A BLOCK OF BEESWAX BEFORE SEWING.

Give yourself aromatherapy treatment while you iron, and subtly scent your clothes into the bargain – dampen your iron-ing with a plant spray full of water to which you have added just a couple of drops of your favourite essential oil. Do what the Spanish señoras do – add a few drops of your favourite *eau de cologne* to the damping water.

THE LINEN CLOSET

In continental Europe, India, China, Russia, and Scandinavia this is not usually a mere "airing cupboard", as in England, but a vast, often highly decorated, piece of furniture where crisp table- and bed-linen is perfumed with a wide array of flowers and insect-repellent herbs and spices. It is most enjoyable to make aromatic little **herb bags** for your linen closet out of fine muslin, lawn, cheesecloth, or fabric scraps (old fashioned mattress and pillow ticking looks very effective against antique lace), but if you haven't the time sprinkle a few drops of lavender, cedar, sandalwood, patchouli, rosemary, or thyme oil on cotton wool

Vrouw den Hollander's Moth-Repellent Sachets

1 CUP DRIED THYME

½ CUP GRATED DRIED ORANGE PEEL

1 CUP DRIED MINT LEAVES

½ CUP DRIED PENNYROYAL

1 TSP GROUND CINNAMON

1 CUP CORIANDER SEEDS, BRUISED

½ CUP ORRIS ROOT POWDER

If you prefer less spicy mixtures, try this 17th-century English "sweet bagge" concoction, traditionally stuffed into drawstring bags made of pastel-hued taffeta:

Faerie Fol-De-Rols

1 CUP EACH DRIED ROSEBUDS, HYSSOP, AND WOODRUFF

½ CUP DRIED SOUTHERNWOOD

1 CUP DRIED LEMON VERBENA OR LEMON BALM

½ CUP NON-IODIZED ROCK SALT

balls and leave them in the corners of the closet, or scatter little tied bunches of lavender stems between folded sheets. A handful of cloves, ground peppercorns, and allspice berries on a saucer not only fragrances the air but repels insects and absorbs damp.

TO MAKE A SWEET-BAGGE FOR LINENN

"Take of Orris roses, sweet Calamus, cypress roots, of dried Lemon-peel, and dried Orange peel; of each a pound, a peck of dried roses: make all these into a gross powder, coriander seed four ounces, nutmegs an ounce and a half, an ounce of cloves; make all these into fine powder and mix with the other; add musk and ambergris; then take four large handfuls of lavender-flowers dried and rubbed; of sweet marjoram, orange leaves, and young walnut leaves, of each a handful, all dried and rubb'd; mix all together, with some bits of cotton perfum'd with essences, and put it up into silk bags to lay with your Linnen."

THE COMPLEAT HOUSEWIFE

If you are storing delicate white fabrics, wrapping them in blue tissue paper protects them from light, which will yellow them. Valuable antique materials such as heritage quilts should be stored in acid-free tissue-paper. Coloured silks and ribbons are traditionally stored in thick, coarse brown paper to preserve their bright hues. Ideally a linen closet should have slatted shelves to allow air to circulate freely. Don't pack your linen too tightly or it will not be able to "breathe" and will crease badly. Slip moth-repellent sachets between layers and folds of material (see left).

The Mending Basket

Dried coffee grounds inside your **pincushion** keep the pins from rusting. Rubbed dry lavender is also an excellent non-rust filling. Keep a little magnet in your workbasket to pick up dropped pins. Bent **needles** can be straightened by dipping them in very hot water. When you have satisfactorily straightened them, dip them in cold water. If you are having trouble threading your needle, hold the eye of the needle against something white.

Make improvised **thimbles** out of the cut off finger-tops of worn-out rubber gloves, and use an old lightbulb as an emergency darning mushroom. Eyebrow tweezers are perfect for removing tiny unwanted stitches. Second-hand shops are wonderful sources of perfectly good zips, interesting old buttons, and old-fashioned remnants for patchwork.

Rubbing your button cotton over a block of beeswax is an old tailor's trick that makes the thread much stronger (see also p.107). Another useful old hint is preventing **tangling** when sewing with double thread by knotting each strand separately.

Don't forget to soak patchwork pieces in very hot water before you use them or you will find that when you wash your quilt the pieces may shrink, with unfortunate results.

"Here's fine Lavender for your cloaths! Here's your sweet Lavender Sixteen springs for a penny – Which you will find my ladies Will smell as sweet as any."

LONDON STREET CRY

"Silks, when washed, should be dried in the shade, on a linen-horse, taking care that they are kept smooth and unwrinkled. If black or blue, they will be improved if laid again on the table, when dry, and sponged with gin, or whiskey, or other white spirit."

DUTIES OF THE LAUNDRY-MAID,

MRS BEETON'S BOOK OF HOUSEHOLD MANAGEMENT

The BATHROOM

> *"Thy baths shall be the juice of July-flowers,*
> *Spirit of roses, and of violets,*
> *The milk of unicorns, and panthers' breath*
> *Gathered in bags, and mixed with Cretan wines."*
>
> VOLPONE, BEN JONSON

The bathroom and toilet are often the only truly private places in the house. It is hardly any wonder then that the current trend in interior design is (space allowing) to make them both seem less functional and more like proper rooms to unwind in. Baths can be made to seem larger by enclosing them in tiled or plastered stepped platforms which cry out to be dotted with candles, burning incense, and a goblet of wine or two. The toilet, as long as it can be kept clean and fresh, does not have to be a neutral, utilitarian cupboard, but can have its horizons expanded with a home-made contemplative or exotic mural, offset by sweet odours of antiseptic herbs.

These "forgotten" living spaces are the places where you can be as original and creative as you like – you can paint a dull chest of drawers a luminous colour and top it with a slab of marble – hey presto – it becomes a towel-cum-toilet-roll store and washstand rolled into one. You can make your bathroom conjure up the islands of Greece by using pure bleached icing-sugar white and dazzling cerulean blue natural pigment paint, with bright china fragments, shells, and pebbles set in cement for the sink splashback. On the shelves – rows of interestingly shaped bottles full of home-made herbal unguents and lotions, sweetie-coloured tinctures, and dishes heaped with spicy washballs and rainbow-coloured cubes of home-made soap.

HAIR TREATMENTS
NASTURTIUM LEAVES, SEEDS
AND FLOWERS, ALL RICH IN
SULPHUR, ARE WIDELY USED
IN FRANCE IN HOME-MADE
SHAMPOOS AND
HAIR-TONICS.

IN RUSSIA AND
SCANDINAVIA FOLK-
RECIPES FOR DANDRUFF
UTILIZE BIRCH LEAVES.

Zen-like austerity is more a feature of Japanese bathroom design – the simple mulberry-leaf sliding screens, the raked gravel (symbolizing water) indoor flower-bed containing rustling bamboo. . . and then – surprise, surprise – the large shallow bath full of family members sitting chatting!

> *"Eighteen bushels of ashes, one bushel of stone lime, three pounds of tallow, fifteen pounds of the purest Bombay wax of a lovely green color, and a peck of salt."*
> SOAP RECIPE SENT TO BENJAMIN FRANKLIN BY HIS SISTER, LIVING IN ENGLAND

Cleansing the body is done before one enters the water, for the bath, for the Japanese, is for relaxation, energy renewal, and family bonding, not for actual ablution. Many cultures: Indian, Scandinavian, and Native American, for example, see the act of plunging into water as a cleansing, spiritual act quite separate from washing. Sweating in a sauna created by pouring water on red-hot stones, followed by an icy dip is an ancient Viking ritual. Native Americans favour a tradition of purification via sweat-lodges presided over by a shaman, as well as steam baths in which the participants crouch naked over a pot of simmering herbs, usually containing aromatic goldenrod.

It wasn't until the 1880s that plumbed baths were invented, but the idea of personal cleanliness symbolizing spiritual purity and physical health has been around for thousands of years. Ancient Greece was proud of its "sanctuaries"; shrines full of bathing pools filled by spring water blessed by the god of healing – Asklepios. In Ancient Rome people did not have their own bathrooms – they visited vast public baths such as the Baths of Caracalla in Rome, where 1600 people at a time could engage in any number of cleansing activities: scraping the dirt and sweat off with a sickle-shaped instrument called a strigil, and plunging into the frigidium, or icy-cold pool, or stewing in the oven-hot sudatorium bathing hall.

(Previous page)
"Our sister – water, very serviceable and humble, and precious and clean."
ST FRANCIS OF ASSISI

The Celtic Ancient Britons were not quite so passionate about washing, but in their theology water was a portal to the Otherworld. Willow trees were tied with "prayer-rags", whose messages and entreaties were carried across the water to the beyond. The faithful drew a Druidic spiral on their foreheads with the sacred water to send the prayer on its journey.

Cleopatra, and Poppea, the wife of Emperor Nero, were partial to bathing in perfumed asses' milk. Madame de Pompadour liked her bath-milk enlivened with honey, lavender, and rose-petals, while Mary Queen of Scots preferred to wash in red wine rather than drink it. Ancient history is rich with recipes for bath-time health and beauty regimens, including an anti-spot mask made of pulverized birds' nests from Ovid; a foot- and elbow-pumicing bathtime treatment from the beauty-box of Queen Thutu, 1400 BC; a Turkish bath-time delight made of mashed rose petals; and a ground-ivy anti-ageing face mask used by American Southern belles.

English medieval ladies of high rank bathed monthly in canvas-lined baths screened by painted canopies. However, in later European history even royalty bathed the whole body extremely rarely, preferring to drench themselves in perfume and strap bags of herbs under their arms to mask pungent body odour. Henry VIII insisted that his palaces be sprinkled with musk perfume to overwhelm rank wafts from his courtiers. At Versailles, Louis XIV washed his hands and face daily in spirits of wine, but ignored his nether regions. It did not help public cleanliness that in the reign of England's Charles I commercial soap was heavily taxed; this excise duty was not removed until the 19th century.

The idea that splashing about in water is good for you didn't really catch on in England until the Victorian era, the Golden Age of Plumbing. One of the bizarre inventions of the day was the "velo-douche" (bike-shower), which recycled the water to the shower-head as one cycled! Until well after the 1950s in England, those with modest means still bathed in tin baths by the fire or stove, the entire family using the same water. In

HAIR WASHING TIPS
CORNFLOUR SPRINKLED ON TO GREASY HAIR IS AN EXCELLENT DRY SHAMPOO.

CIDER VINEGAR IN THE FINAL RINSE MAKES HAIR GLOSSY AND GETS RID OF ALKALINE SOAP RESIDUE.

NETTLES STEEPED IN THE VINEGAR WORK WONDERS ON DANDRUFF.

KEEP SHAMPOO OUT OF LITTLE CHILDREN'S EYES BY PUTTING A THICK BARRIER OF VASELINE ON THEIR FOREHEADS.

(Overleaf)
"The steam circled in ghostly eddies, and the candle paled in the haze …The cake of soap mingling its own intimate smell with the strong aromatic odour of hot rainwater."
COUNTRY HOARD, ALISON UTTLEY, 1943

SIMON THE SCENTED
SOAP SQUID
BUNCH TOGETHER THE
CENTRE OF A SOFT OLD
FLANNEL, STUFF IT WITH
OATMEAL, PURE UNSCENTED
SOAP SCRAPS, AND
CHAMOMILE OR LAVENDER
FLOWERS. SECURE WITH A
CONTRASTING-COLOURED
RIBBON, SEW ON SMALL
BUTTONS FOR EYES AND
ARRANGE THE REMAINDER
OF THE FLANNEL AS
"TENTACLES".

Australian pioneer days when water-conservation was of primary importance, families lucky enough to have a creek near by bathed in it all year round, hanging their home-made wire soap-holders from conveniently located nearby gum-trees. When Arnhem Land Aboriginal women bathe in the creeks they use "soap" made from the passion-fruit vine and sing to the "Gurraymi" (women's spirit).

According to the ancient Chinese art of mystical interior design, Feng Shui, mirrors are highly recommended in bathrooms because they are thought to promote the *chi*, or life-force. In this geomantic philosophy, a distorted image in any mirror is highly inadvisable, as the life-force is deflected. Whatever your reflections on the look and atmosphere of your toilet and bathroom – whether they conjure a Chinese shrine, a clapboard seaside chalet, or a baroque boudoir, they should be concerned with using ecologically friendly cleansers and water conservation.

Many "state-of-the-art" modern cleaning fluids are hazardous to the human respiratory system and enamel or porcelain-ware alike. As for water use, showers use far less than a bath, especially if you have a low-flow head instead of a power-shower. Mending one dripping tap could save up to 600 bathfuls of water per year. Together, the bath and toilet use up to seventy percent of the domestic water supply in Britain, while in North America families use up to an amazing 48 litres (220 gallons) per day! Part of this frightening figure comes from the toilet flush, which in America can use up to 22 litres (5 gallons) with each use. In England and most of Europe the volume is more like 10 litres (2.9 gallons). This can be lessened by installing a low-level flush cistern, or putting a small (well-sealed) bag of sand in the cistern, well away from the ball-cock mechanism.

In Scandinavia and Germany the water-less compost lavatory is increasingly popular, not unlike a somewhat sophisticated version of the English country privy and the Australian outback "dunny" of yesteryear. At the Centre for Alternative Technology in Wales research is also proceeding into a natural filtration sewage plant using reedbeds which recycles effluent to drinking water purity; as well as a system which allows households to re-utilize their bathwater to water the garden.

As in the bathroom, keep plants on the windowsill in the toilet, as their transpiration process helps keep the air fresh. Our ancestors, of course, mainly relieved themselves in the open air, using moss, leaves and, robustly, shells. Toilet paper was a Chinese invention which didn't take America and Europe by storm until late this century. It was Queen Elizabeth I's godson Sir John Harington who invented the water-closet in 1596 in order that "unsavoury places may be made sweet". The "Ajax" (a pun on the Elizabethan "jakes", or privy) cost thirty shillings and eight-pence and boasted a magnificently unhygienic red velvet seat. Her Majesty was given the prototype gratis, and had it installed at Richmond Palace under lock and key.

HONEY BEE SEED-SOAP

2 AVERAGE-SIZED BARS OF
PURE WHITE SOAP, GRATED
1 TBSP HONEY
4 DROPS OF CARAWAY
ESSENTIAL OIL
2 DROPS OF CARDAMOM
ESSENTIAL OIL
2 TSP OF
CARAWAY SEEDS

Gently melt the soap and honey in a double-boiler/bain-marie, and put in the oils and seeds. Mix well. Pour into a mould lined with greaseproof paper. Leave about two weeks to harden.

ELIZABETHAN BATH VINEGAR

1 CUP HIGHLY SCENTED DRIED PELARGONIUM LEAVES
A SMALL BOTTLE CIDER VINEGAR
3 DROPS ROSE GERANIUM ESSENTIAL OIL
2 DROPS NEROLI ESSENTIAL OIL

Steep the leaves in the cider vinegar and leave in a warm place for a couple of weeks. Strain, add the oils, and re-bottle in an exotic-looking glass phial. A splash under the running tap turns your bath into an aroma-water-therapy paradise.

"Queen Caroline
Washed her face
with turpentine.
Turpentine will
make it shine,
Poor Queen Caroline."
TRADITIONAL
ENGLISH RHYME

SOAP

It is said that Roman women "discovered" soap some 3000 years ago by accident when they were washing some sacred stones after an animal sacrifice. The combination of fat, water, and ashes from the sacrificial fire created a crude soapy substance. Traditional soap-making, utilizing as it does spluttering fat (many folk recipes from Europe, America, and Australia incorporate tallow, suet, and "breakfast grease") plus caustic lye – an alkaline solution made by water dripping through wood ash, is a dangerous operation.

SIMPLE TOOTHPASTE

3 TBSP ORRIS ROOT

3 TBSP BICARBONATE
OF SODA

3 DROPS PEPPERMINT OIL

Mix together and store in an
airtight container. Sprinkle on
to a damp toothbrush.

THE MOST SIMPLE
TOOTHPOWDER OF ALL IS
BICARBONATE OF SODA.

LADY VENETIA'S WONDROUS WASH-BALLS

2 AVERAGE-SIZED BARS OF GLYCERINE OR
UNSCENTED PURE SOAP, GRATED
1 CUP FINE OATMEAL
3 TBSP RUBBED LAVENDER FLOWERS, FINELY CHOPPED
DRIED EAU DE COLOGNE MINT AND ROSE PETALS
1 CUP ROSE-WATER
3 DROPS LAVENDER OIL & 3 DROPS CLOVE OIL

Put the soap in a bowl with the other ingredients except the rose
water, which you heat, and pour over the mixture. Stir and leave
for fifteen minutes, then squish together until the ingredients
are evenly distributed and there are no lumps. You may need to
melt the mixture a little over hot water in a double saucepan.
Roll into small balls and wrap in greaseproof paper. After a few
days rub the soaps with a little more rose-water to smooth their
surfaces, then store them once more in their papers.

It is far more enjoyable to avoid that corrosive process and
make, instead, your own soap creations using either grated pure
soap with your own additions (essential oils, oatmeal, carrot oil)
or recycled soap scraps. In 16th- and 17th-century England
"wash balls" were commonly used in well-to-do households for
cleansing face and hands. Made of left-over slivers of expensive
Spanish soap imported from Castile, plus stale bread, honey,
herbs, and spices, these round brown soaps were fragranced with
spicy oils and used to scent stored gloves and clothing when not
in use at the wash-basin.

TUNISIAN TABLETS

2 CUPS COLOURED SOAP SCRAPS
2 DROPS EACH JASMINE, TANGERINE,
AND GINGER ESSENTIAL OILS
1 TSP GLYCERINE

Collect small pieces of brightly coloured soap.
Put them in a bain-marie with rose essential oil
and a few drops of glycerine, then mix it to a rain-
bow sludge. When this has softened,
let it cool a bit then pour into moulds lined with
grease-proof paper. Leave for two weeks to dry.

BATHROOM CLEANING

The best way of regulating bathroom **humidity** is to keep plants by the window (keep open as much as possible for good ventilation). Porous, hard-wearing surfaces such as cork and naturally waxed timber help condensation, as does "breathing" organic paint. Cotton, linen, or muslin curtains are also excellent humidity absorbers. Cane and wicker furniture originally designed for, and still used in, tropical climates, as well as seagrass or rush matting, positively thrive in a damp atmosphere.

Many of the bewildering array of bathroom cleansers on the market use either chlorine or ammonia, which when mixed give off a highly toxic gas. There are simple, cheap biodegradable alternatives sitting in your kitchen cupboard.

SHOWERS

The most ergonomic way of cleaning the shower is to get family members to do it while they're actually using it! Keep a soft old scourer or specially designated nailbrush near the soap-dish, along with bicarbonate of soda and a bottle of vinegar. A quick scrub with the former and a sluice with the latter decimates soap scum and mouldy grouting. Blockages caused by hair and soap build-up down the plug-hole can often be solved with a wire coat-hanger bent into a spiral.

Clean **shower-heads** covered with lime-scale with a cup of hot vinegar and salt. Leave this strong natural acid solution on only until the scale begins to dislodge, then quickly rinse it off. If the encrustation is blocking the holes take the head apart and poke a large needle through each in turn.

Mildewed **shower-curtains** are most unappetizing. Scrub them thoroughly with bicarbonate of soda mixed with lemon juice. Before they are re-hung soak them for an hour in salted water.

MIRRORS

A low-level mirror in the bathroom is a great incentive to children for washing, teeth-cleaning, and hair-combing. You can

HERBS FOR THE BATH

A TIME-HONOURED WAY OF MAKING AN EMOLLIENT HERB-BAG FOR THE BATH IS TO PUT A TABLESPOON OF DRIED HERBS OF YOUR CHOICE (ROSEMARY, ELDER-FLOWERS, MINT LEAVES, SINGLY OR MIXED) IN A LITTLE MUSLIN BAG ALONG WITH A TABLESPOON OF OATMEAL. TIE OR SEW TIGHTLY, AND SWISH IT ABOUT UNDER THE RUNNING TAP (AN UPLIFTING SOUND) BEFORE YOU GET IN AND RELAX.

prevent mirrors from fogging up when you are running the bath by putting the cold water in first. Alternatively, rub the mirror with a few drops of detergent, shampoo or glycerine. Remember that steam affects the silvering of old mirrors very badly. Make sure that the back is well sealed, and fix it away from the wall to allow air to circulate behind. (See also p.29.)

BATHS AND SINKS

Rust stains on baths respond well to a rub with borax and lemon juice made into a paste, or cream of tartar. Treat unsightly green **limescale** drip stains with hot vinegar. Buttermilk left to soak in for half an hour or so often works as well. Miscellaneous other marks usually come off enamel after a vigorous rub with a mix of half natural turps and half linseed, or natural turps and salt on a washleather or soft cloth, rinsed off with soapy water. Don't use this on a plastic bath or you will harm the surface.

Mould-filled sink overflows can be best attacked with an old child-size toothbrush coated with borax, or lemon juice or vinegar and bicarbonate of soda. To shine up **chrome** and **brass taps** rub on salt and vinegar to make them gleam. Let the solution dry before buffing with a washleather.

PAINTWORK AND TILES

Restore glossy bathroom **paintwork** to its pristine shininess with a solution of pure soap flakes and milk. Clean specked **tiles** with a cut lemon, and rub down well with a soft cloth. To make them glossy, wipe with milky water, rinse, and then buff. Once again, old toothbrushes come in handy for cleaning grouting and all those other fiddly places.

SPONGES AND FLANNELS

To prevent your flannels and natural sponges from becoming slimy with soap residues, soak them once a week in a solution of half vinegar and half hot water. The vinegar does not leave a lingering smell, but if you want your sponge to be scented put a few drops of lavender oil in the water.

"Take Sage, Lavender flowers, Rose flowers of each two handfuls, and a little salt, boil them in water and make a bath not too hot in which to bathe the Body in a morning, or two hours before meat."

FIVE HUNDRED RECEIPTS, JOHN MIDDLETON, 1734

BATHMATS

You can make colourful bathmats from strips of old towels and discarded towelling dressing gowns sewn together (look in charity shops and second-hand sales). Stand them on a wooden duckboard to prevent them becoming damp and smelly.

TOILET CLEANING

This is the room where the chemical cocktail is often the strongest – any number of bleaching "super-cleansers" swooshed down the U-bend, odour- and foam-releasers clamped under the rim, and "floral" aerosol sprays and fake wood-curl "pot-pourri" utilized for good measure. Wholesome old-fashioned cleaning measures, a germicidal pot-pourri on the windowsill and regular spraying with a plant-mister filled with water and 10 drops of anti-bacterial and insect repellant tea-tree oil will keep the room fresh and pleasant.

Sea-glass is very pretty and retains odours well. Put a collection in a bowl and sprinkle with 15 drops of antiseptic rosemary or thyme oil. To make sure each piece of glass has absorbed some oil, turn with a spoon for a minute or two. Put in a tall clear jar on a shelf or windowsill in the toilet.

If you've just moved into a new home to be greeted by an unpleasant **lime-scale**-encrusted toilet bowl, give it an overnight face-pack of flour and hot vinegar (the flour keeps the vinegar in place). In the morning an attack with a wire-brush and a few vigorous flushes should make it pristine. Borax and lemon-juice also work well on stained bowls. Clean the seat regularly with a cup of bicarbonate of soda, a cup of warm vinegar, and six drops of lavender oil. Rinse well.

"Clean hands and hearts may hope
To find the way to happiness
By using lots of soap."
SLOGAN OF THE AMERICAN CLEANLINESS INSTITUTE, 1924

QUEEN VICTORIA'S POTENT
POT-POURRI
1 CUP EACH DRIED
LAVENDER FLOWERS
AND DRIED FRAGRANT
ROSE PETALS
1 CUP EACH DRIED THYME
LEAVES AND DRIED CISTUS
LEAVES AND PETALS
2 DROPS EACH JUNIPER ROSE-
WOOD, AND CITRONELLA
ESSENTIAL OILS
1 TBSP CLOVES
1 CUP SEA SALT

The ATTIC & CELLAR

*"What a museum of curiosities is the garret of
a well-regulated New England house."*

THE STORY OF A BAD BOY, THOMAS BAILEY ALDRICH,

BOSTON, 1870

Literature loves attics, thinks of them as escape havens where the rain patters musically on the roof. Think of Jo in *Little Women,* gorging herself up in her secret eyrie on dreams, sweet, wrinkled apples, and good books. At the same time spare a thought for the poor governess in Henry James' *Turn of the Screw,* realizing, among the dusty discarded toys and old trunks, that there may be something sinister going on at the manor. The room at the very top of any house often has the feel of an atmospheric, almost magical, place. It often has a far-reaching, top-of-the-world view over rooftops or countryside, and can seem like a sort of architectural time-machine, full of eerily juxtaposed relics of ours and other people's yesteryears.

Traditionally in the country it has been more of a stillroom or store-room overflow: a place for drying and storing apples in the winter, for festooning drying herbs and flowers scenting the room with summer. The common image of the attic is of a rough chamber cluttered with jumble, but in Shaker buildings they were as exquisitely finished as the rest of the house – full of wonderful poplar and pine units for storing out-of-season clothing. At the Church Farm Dwelling, Canterbury, New Hampshire, the immaculate attic contained six closets, 14 cupboards, and 101 drawers. Another at Enfield boasted 860 drawers, all numbered and labelled!

PLANTING HOUSELEEK (COUNTRY NAME: WELCOME-HOME HUSBAND THOUGH NEVER SO DRUNK), OR STONECROP, ON THE ROOF WAS THOUGHT TO GIVE THE HOUSE PROTECTION AGAINST LIGHTNING AND FIRE.

More and more people in contemporary times are utilizing some or all of the space as an extra bedroom/play-room/meditation space, or hobby room. Many modern Scandinavian houses are left open-plan internally right up to the roof space, with galleries and sleeping platforms connected by swooping wooden walkways. In the long, cold northern winters the houses are given extra insulation by the deep layer of snow on the roof.

In Britain the houses are sometimes unhealthy and energy-inefficient because of both inadequate ventilation and insulation up in the attic spaces. It has been estimated that at least half of the heat loss in homes is due to inadequate insulation. The most human and environmentally friendly insulation to buy is probably cellulose fibre made from recycled newsprint. Many alternatives are manufactured from polystyrene, releasing CFC gases. Lagging hot-water pipes with rags or ancient woollies prevents them from freezing in an icy winter. Similarly, lagging your hot-water tank keeps the heat from being lost through the roof space. A well-fitting cylinder is important, but you can help it along with old blankets and sleeping bags.

Without enough ventilation in the attic your house, especially if it is centrally heated and double-glazed, will be hermetically sealed, and therefore completely unable to "breathe". The attic itself will undoubtedly have condensation problems, which is an invitation for mildews and moulds to activate. It is commonly thought these days that their airborne spores may trigger asthma and eczema allergies, as well as causing harm to your stored treasures and oddments.

(Previous page)
"Ever since the habitations of men were reared two storeys high has the garret been the nursery of genius."
THE IDLE THOUGHTS OF AN IDLE FELLOW,
JEROME K. JEROME, 1889

The first thing to do is to check thoroughly that any vents you might have under the eaves are not completely blocked by insulating material. Any dormer or skylight windows should be left open a crack – not wide enough for bats and birds to get in, though. In some countries bats are a protected species, so if you do find that they have roosted in your roofspace, contact a bat conservation trust or similar organization (see pp.136-7), or your local conservation officer, or equivalent.

The bat is of course one of the most powerful images in folk mythology. Australian Aboriginals and many black African peoples believe that bats are representative of man's soul – and that to kill one is very bad luck indeed. But perhaps the universally best-known of attic superstitions concern fertility, specifically the storing of baby clothes. Many women refuse to throw away long outgrown tiny jackets and bonnets in the firm folk belief that to do so would almost certainly result in pregnancy. Alternatively, anyone who stores anything made of peacock feathers will not, according to folk myth, have children, because of the "evil eye" symbol on the feathers.

Some people have an irrational nervousness of cellars, thinking of them as Hades-dark caves dripping with water. Today many imaginative families have transformed their "underworld" areas into teenage dens, workshops, and additional pantries. Despite the cellar's poor general image, the well-regulated household of the past kept this room sweet and fresh with regular white-washing and damp-treatment. Which is just as well as this is where the household water-filtering jars, ice-boxes, vegetables, and meat-safes were kept.

It was generally believed that the combination of standing water and rotting veg led to "poisonous miasmas", so housekeepers were rigorous about cleanliness and drainage. Whether your cellar is just big enough to hold a few shelves of chutney jars and pots of narcissi bulbs or is like a subterranenan ballroom, the same rules apply.

A highly energy-efficient boiler is a must – among its other jobs it helps to keep the cellar sound and dry. Also the walls should not be covered with a non-permeable synthetic coating, or the naturally present moisture will just find its way out elsewhere! Plenty of ventilation helps to solve damp. As with the attic or loft, check that you have no toxic timber treatments (a simple borax solution works just as well), and no old asbestos fire-proofing. In Victorian times coal was always kept in the cellar, shot under ground from the street through a man-hole. One of the rules of

"Twinkle twinkle little bat!
How I wonder what you're at!
Up above the world you fly,
Like a tea-tray in the sky."
ALICE IN WONDERLAND,
LEWIS CARROLL, 1865

THE CELLAR IS THE USUAL PLACE TO FIND THE COAL STORE, AS LIGHT MAKES COAL CHUNKS CRUMBLE TO DUST. IN VICTORIAN TIMES, FRUGAL HOUSEHOLDERS THREW A BUCKET OF WATER IN WHICH A HANDFUL OF WASHING SODA HAD BEEN DISSOLVED OVER THE NEW COAL DELIVERY. THEY THEN ONLY USED IT WHEN IT HAD DRIED. THIS ODD RITUAL MADE THE COAL BURN FOR LONGER.

the popular "First Footer" New Year's Eve good luck superstitions was that the symbolic coal carried by the first dark-haired man over the threshold on the stroke of midnight had to be brought with him in his pocket, not just carried upstairs and handed over for the occasion.

SOAP JELLY

1 HANDFUL LEFTOVER SOAP BITS

1 TSP WASHING SODA

BOILING, SOFT RAIN WATER

Shred soap into a large jar, add the washing soda and fill up the jar with boiling water. When it is cool it will have become a lovely squidgy jelly suitable for cleaning all kinds of delicate objects.

THE ATTIC

If it is warmish, airy and accessible, this is an excellent place to dry **herbs** and **flowers** (see also p.39). As in the kitchen, make sure that the herbs are secured in small bunches, hanging "head first", though not in direct light, and protected from dust and mildew spores in brown paper bags with the bottoms cut off, to aid circulation of the air.

If you are hanging up seedheads, don't forget to put a non-open-weave receptacle underneath to catch the falling seeds! Check your drying stock regularly and remove any that are smelling musty and looking damp.

If you are drying flowers on racks, give them a gentle shake every now and then and keep them covered with muslin or cheesecloth to stop them getting dusty. When your petals or flowers are completely dry, keep them in airtight containers until you are ready to use them.

The attic is also the traditional place to dry and store apples. They must be unblemished before you place them on racks, and must not touch each other at all. Check them every week and take out any which have developed any specks and bruises.

> *"The attic was a lovely place to play. The large, round, coloured pumpkins made beautiful chairs and tables. The red peppers and onions dangled overhead. The hams and the venison hung in their paper wrappings, and all the bunches of dried herbs, the spicy herbs for cooking and the bitter herbs for medicine, gave the place a dusty-spicy smell."*
>
> LITTLE HOUSE IN THE BIG WOODS,
> LAURA INGALLS WILDER

TO PRESERVE BOOKS

"Russian leather, which is perfumed with the tar of birch tree, never moulders; and merchants suffer large bales of this leather to remain in the London docks, knowing that it cannot sustain any injury from damp.
This manner of preserving books with perfumed oils was known to the Ancients. The Romans used oil of cedar to preserve valuable manuscripts."

THE ENGLISHWOMAN'S
DOMESTIC MAGAZINE, 1853

You can hang **home-made candles** at attic windows to bleach on a sunny day, but do not leave them hanging there in a heatwave, or you will be left with some bizarre, bendy illuminants!

MILDEW

Combating mildew is an ongoing battle in most storage areas. As a rule of thumb it is a good idea not to have pictures, artefacts, or furniture propped up against any external walls where condensation may cause them considerable damage. It is quite easy to get rid of a recent attack on books, papers, and documents by gently brushing it off with a toothbrush. Some people put slightly damp papers in the bottom oven of a cooking range for a few hours, but I wouldn't recommend this with anything that is valuable. Dust cornflour between the pages of paperbacks and then brush off with a soft cloth. If they are stored in a cupboard that has begun to smell like a Dickensian second-hand bookshop, dot cotton wool balls soaked in vanilla essence about and the problem should be eradicated. On no account store anything long-term in a plastic bag, as it will certainly go mouldy.

SAFE STORAGE

For advice on storage of **old books** of monetary, historic, or sentimental value do consult a qualified conservator. The rule of thumb with disintegrating old volumes is not to bind them up

SADDLE SOAP
TAKE QUARTER OF A CUP
OF PURE GRATED SOAP
QUARTER OF A CUP OF BEST
LINSEED OIL,
HALF A CUP OF BEESWAX,
HALF A CUP OF WHITE WINE
OR CIDER VINEGAR.
DISSOLVE THE BEESWAX
GENTLY IN THE VINEGAR
OVER A LOW HEAT,
GRADUALLY ADDING THE
SOAP AND OIL, STIRRING
UNTIL SMOOTH AND
CREAMY. POUR INTO TINS
AND COOL. THE SOLIDIFIED
"SOAP" CAN BE RUBBED ON
TO LEATHER WITH A SOFT
CLOTH AND THEN BUFFED
TO A BRILLIANT SHINE.

with elastic bands or swathes of string, but to wrap them individually in clean paper, ideally acid-free tissue paper, until they can be assessed and repaired by an expert. In the meantime, keep them away from light and away from external walls and stack them in heavy-duty cardboard boxes.

If you are storing old leather furniture or leather trunks in the attic and they become mildewed, sponge them with a little jellied soap (see p.126) and hot water, and rinse well with cold water. Don't polish them until you are sure the leather is completely dry and the mildew has gone. Then use a good saddle soap to nourish and protect the leather to ensure it does not crack. The chrome on old bikes and prams should be given an occasional clean with crumpled silver foil or baking soda on a damp cloth.

INSECTS AND OTHER PESTS
As a rule of thumb, never store furniture with tiny holes in it in the attic unless you know them to be evidence of a very ancient (dead) infestation of **woodworm**. If you have not already treated the problem (see Bushwhacker's Bug Balm, p.68), make up a stern solution of equal parts of methylated spirits and borax crystals and apply it to the insides of the holes with a very fine paint brush. Cracks, crevices, and all unpolished wood such as the undersides of cupboards, chairs, and drawers, are all vulnerable, so check them regularly. Remember, woodworm grubs take three years to hatch, so don't immediately assume that you are in the clear! To get rid of woodworm in cane furniture, submerge it in water for a couple of days.

Make sure that any woollen clothes, carpets, upholstered furniture, or blankets stored in the attic are protected against **moth** by any of the methods mentioned in previous chapters (see pp. 61 and 108), or by laying dried sprigs of santolina (also known as cotton lavender) liberally among the stored articles. Lavender oil or eucalyptus oil in little saucers or on cotton wool balls should be placed in **silverfish** haunts and replaced regularly. Silverfish and woodworm like moist conditions. Check condensation and leaky pipes. A temporary but effective repair for the latter can be achieved by wrapping waterproof garden twine around the bit with the missing washer.

> *"Wee, sleekit, cow'rin', tim'rous beastie,*
> *O what a panic's in they breastie!*
> *Thou need na start awa sae hasty,*
> *Wi' bickering brattle!*
> *I wad be laith to rin an' chase thee,*
> *Wi' murd'ring pattle!"*
>
> TO A MOUSE, BURNS, 1786

Mice love attics because they are often warm, containing plenty of paper, upholstery stuffing, and other insulation material suitable for nest building. Among the many things mice ruin is electric cable, the casing of which they seem to find irresistible. If they don't seem overly perturbed by the peppermint or chillis advised in the Kitchen chapter (see p.37), ruthlessly block up their holes and organize a cats' tea-party (at least four feline guests are recommended). A liberal scattering of pungent aniseed is also well reported, but be careful that your dog doesn't get locked in the attic, for dogs adore the smell of aniseed – it's used for training bloodhounds.

It's a rare house that doesn't have a **wasps' nest** in the attic at some time in its history. Take comfort in the fact that wasps never come back to the same nest the following year. In extreme cases your local pest control officer may have to come and remove the queen wasp from the nest, after which the workers will disperse. In colonial America, householders used to get rid of wasps nesting in the attic by burning the dried leaves of the sweet Joe Pye herb over coals in a chafing dish.

> *"If bees nest in the roof of a house, the girls of that house will not marry."*
>
> OLD ENGLISH PROVERB

(Overleaf)
"A supply of simples should be in every attic. Most roots should be collected late in the fall. Herbs should be gathered while in blossom, dried in the shade and packed at once in paper."
THE POCOMTUCK HOUSEWIFE, MASSACHUSETTS, 1805

"Here is wine,
Alive with sparkles –
never, I aver,
Since Ariadne was
a vintager
So cool a purple."
ENDYMION,
JOHN KEATS, 1818

That cunning hunter the **spider**, with its beautiful, fantastically engineered web is at the centre of many folk mythologies. Its appearance excites irrational terror in some people. In many countries the wanton destruction of cobwebs is thought to be bad luck, as a web is said to have hidden the infant Jesus from Herod's soldiers during the Slaughter of the Innocents. In English folk legend webs are imbued with curative powers for the staunching of bleeding, while in Spain and Germany to deliberately leave at least one web untouched in your house promotes love and well-being among the inhabitants.

The Ancient Greeks believed the spider to be a beautiful young village girl, Arachne, who had been turned into an eight-legged creepy-crawly by the goddess Athena, who was jealous of the girl's superb weaving ability. The Navajo and Hopi peoples both feature "Grandmother Spider" in their creation myths and the Hopi believe that the world began in an underground cavern full of ants, so they think it very bad luck to kill any subterranean insects.

An old-fashioned feather duster is invaluable for the removal of cobwebs. A bamboo cane and a bit of twine makes a useful extension for very high eaves corners.

Creaks and groans
In Scotland, creaking furniture, especially in the attic, signifies a change in the weather. **Squeaky floorboards** in the attic provide great fuel for childish imaginations and ensuing sleepless nights for parents. Sprinkling talcum powder between the boards often helps supernatural footsteps to cease overnight.

THE CELLAR
People often think shudderingly of cellars as dank, damp dungeons, but there is no reason why we should not utilize the space to the full, as our forbears did. Good ventilation ensures that the relative humidity is not so high that mould and mildew spores are encouraged, and that damp is kept at bay. **Damp-proofing** treatments are expensive, utilize toxic materials, and are often

completely unnecessary. Limewash, available from many specialist paint dealers (see pp.136-7), is an ancient and durable wall-coating which allows the underlying brick or stonework to "breathe" and not retain problem-causing moisture and destructive salts. Its natural causticity also helps to keep bugs at bay.

When **limewashing,** or **whitewashing,** a cellar wall, save your temper by tying a large piece of sponge around the handle of the roller or brush to prevent this highly drippy wall-covering from running down your arms.

"That it may please thee to give and preserve to our use the kindly fruits of the earth, so as in due time we may enjoy them..."

THE BOOK OF
COMMON PRAYER

If you go to live in an old house which seems to have a **damp,** mildewy cellar, leave the basement door open and fill the rest of the house with dry heat, ideally by lighting as many fires as there are fireplaces. After a week or so of such treatment you should notice a considerable difference below stairs. If you feel your cellar is still damp, and your fuse-box is located down there, put a rubber mat on the ground in front of it until you are sure that the problem is eradicated. A permanently *in-situ* torch and a length of fusewire are useful things to keep handy. As an anti-damp measure, wooden posts sunk into the ground benefit from being occasionally painted around their base by an equal mixture of powdered charcoal and linseed oil.

The exclusion of light is the cellar's greatest asset as a specialist store-room, as its dark coolness prevents food and drinkstuffs from sprouting and fermenting. If it is a well-ventilated space, and you do not have a pantry upstairs, the cellar is perfect for the storage of bottled fruits and preserves. Root vegetables such as potatoes keep best down here – in boxes or in sacks of earth, or covered with clean straw. Check them at least once a week to make sure that they are not spoiling.

Wine

The cellar's best-known traditional role is for **wine storage,** as light deteriorates it. To do its job properly, the cellar needs to be dry and draught-free, and at a constant temperature of between 50-60 degrees F (10-15 degrees C). The wine must be stored in

"Some chirurgeons there be that cure warts in this manner; they take a spider's web, rolling the same up on a round heap like a ball, and laying it upon the wart; they then set fire on it and burn it to ashes."

HISTORY OF FOUR-FOOTED

BEASTS AND SERPENTS,

E. TOPSEL, 1607

(Facing page)
"In the cellar, besides the bins of apples and potatoes, the piles of squash, turnip and cabbage lying on the uncovered ground, there are cupboards and shelves full of canned and preserved fruits."

THE COUNTRY KITCHEN,

DELLA LUTES, 1938

a lying-down position, so that the wine remains in permanent contact with the cork. **Fortified wines** can be similarly stored horizontally until a few days before you want to drink them – when they must be brought upstairs and stood upright to allow sediment to fall to the bottom of the bottle.

PESTS

Rats cannot abide the catnip herb. If you see one sniffing about, sprinkle catnip liberally near its entrance/exit point. Alternatively or additionally, make some balls of newspaper, soak them in eucalyptus oil and poke them into any suspected holes. Whether you are successful or otherwise, it is a wise precaution to alert the local pest controller for thorough rat eradication. For getting rid of **beetles** an old tip from the 1950s from the National Federation of Women's Institutes is to cut cucumber rind into slices and place it in their holes to drive them away.

Rat Rhyme
"Rats and mice,
Leave this poor person's house,
Go on away over to the mill,
And there you'll all get your fill."
TRADITIONAL NOTE LEFT NEAR RODENT HOLES,

SCOTLAND AND NORTHERN ENGLAND

USEFUL ADDRESSES

When writing to any of the following, please enclose a stamped, addressed envelope to ensure reply:

The Herb Society,
134 Buckingham Palace Road,
London SW1W 9SA.
(Publish information sheets on herb-growing and how to create herb-gardens).

The Society For Protection of Ancient Buildings,
37 Spital Square,
London E1 6DY.
(Publish a wide range of excellent pamphlets on how to treat damp, rot, etc. in old buildings/environmentally-friendly way.)

Centre for Alternative Technology,
Llwyngwern Quarry,
Machynlleth,
Powys SY2O 9AZ.
(Have an extensive mail-order book-list on a number of ecological issues relating to the household. Send a large SAE and £1 for the catalogue.)

Waste Watch,
Gresham House,
24 Holborn Viaduct,
London EC1A 2BN.
(Publish bulletins and information pamphlets on recycling issues.)

Ecological Design Association,
2O High Street,
Stroud,
Glos GL5 1AS.
(Publish EcoDesign magazine and maintain lists of eco-architects.)

Bat Conservation Trust
15 Cloisters House,
8 Battersea Park Rd,
London SW8 4BG.

London Ecology Centre,
45 Shelton St,
London WC2H 9HJ.
(The Centre is an information unit with a "World of Difference" shop selling a wide variety of household eco-products. Mail order).

SUPPLIERS

G. Baldwin & Co,
173 Walworth Road,
London SE17 1RW.
(Delightfully old-fashioned herbalists in apothecary-style shop. Dried herbs, beeswax, essential oils, pot-pourri fixatives, home-made cosmetics ingredients etc. Mail order.)

Culpeper Ltd,
Hadstock Road,
Linton,
Cambs CB1 6NJ.
(HQ and mail-order outlet.)

Napiers Herbalists,
Forrest Bank,
Barr,
Ayrshire KA26 9TN,
Scotland.
(Mail order outlet of the long-established Edinburgh herbalists. Also sell essential oils.)

Bay House Aromatics,
88 St George's Rd,
Brighton,
E. Sussex BN2 1EE.
(Essential oil specialists. Mail order.)

Barwinnock Herbs,
Barrhill,
Ayrshire KA26 OTB,
Scotland.

(Specialist nursery for a comprehensive range of medicinal, household and cosmetic herbs. Mail order.)

Suffolk Herbs Ltd,
Monks Farm,
Coggeshall Road,
Kelvedon,
Essex CO5 9PG.
(Herb and ornamental flower seeds, plus herbal products. Mail order.)

The Little Green Shop,
16 Gardner St,
Brighton BN1 1UP.
(Environmentally-friendly, green household products. Mail order.)

Auro Organic Paint Supplies,
Unit 1,
Goldstone Farm,
Ashdon,
Saffron Walden,
Essex CB1O 2L2.
(Mail order.)

Potmolen Paints (Traditional & Natural Paints),
27 Woodcock Industrial Estate,
Warminster,
Wilts BA12 9DX.

(Wide range of old-fashioned, sound paint-products, waxes, timber treatments etc. Restoration consultancy. Mail order.)

Crucial Trading,
The Market Hall,
Craven Arms,
Shrops SY7 9NY.
(Traditional, natural flooring materials: coir, jute, sisal, sea-grass, "medieval matting" etc. Mail order.)

Shaker,
25 Harcourt St,
London W1H 1DT.
(Shaker products and many interesting books on Shaker and Amish life and art. Mail order.)

Falkiner Fine Papers Ltd,
76 Southampton Row,
London WC1B 4AR
(Supply conservation-grade acid-free tissue paper and many other restoration materials. Mail order.)

Caurnie Soaperie,
Kirkintilloch G66 1QZ,
Scotland.
(Manufacturers of completely pure unperfumed soap, not tested on animals. Mail order.)

SELECTED BIBLIOGRAPHY

Five Hundred Pointes of Good Husbandrie, Thomas Tusser, 1573

The English Housewife, Gervase Markham, 1683

The Closet of Sir Kenelm Digby Opened, 1669

The Gentlewoman's Companion, Hannah Woolley, 1675

The Countrie Housewife's Garden, William Lawson, 1617

The Dictionary of Daily Wants, Houlston and Wright, London, 1861

Grandmother's Household Hints, Helen Lyon Adamson, Frederick Muller, 1965

Our Own Snug Fireside - Images of the New England Home 1760-1860, Jane C. Nylander, Yale University Press, 1994

Shaker Life, Work and Art, Jane Sprigg and David Larkin, Cassell, 1987

The National Trust Book of Forgotten Household Crafts, John Seymour, Dorling Kindersley, 1987

The Foxfire Books, 1 & 2, ed. Eliot Wigginton, Anchor Books, New York, 1972/3

A Woman's Work is Never Done: A History of Housework in the British Isles 1650-1950, Caroline Davidson, Chatto & Windus, 1982

Pioneer Women of the Bush and Outback, Jennifer Isaacs, Lansdowne Press, Sydney, 1990

Bush Food: Aboriginal Food and Herbal Medicine, Jennifer Isaacs, Lansdowne Press, 1988

A Modern Herbal, Mrs. M. Grieve, Jonathan Cape, 1931

The Complete Herbal, Geraldene Holt, Conran Octopus, 1991

The Illustrated Earth Garden Herbal, Keith Vincent Smith, Elm Tree, 1978.

The Royal Horticultural Society Encyclopaedia of Herbs and Their Uses, Deni Brown, Dorling Kindersley, 1995.

Plants With A Purpose, Richard Mabey, Collins, 1977.

A Dictionary of Superstitions, ed. Iona Opie and Moira Tatem, Oxford Unversity Press, 1992

Encylopaedia of Superstitions, E & M.A. Radford, ed./revised Christina Hole, Hutchinson, 1961

Superstitions, Peter Lorie, Simon & Schuster, New York, 1992

Wildflower Folklore, Laura C. Martin, The East Woods Press, North Carolina

The Green Home, Karen Christensen, Piatkus, 1995

The Natural House Book, David Pearson, Gaia/Conran Octopus, 1989

The Fragrant Pharmacy, Valerie ann Worwood, Bantam, 1990

Grandmother's Secrets, Jean Palaiseul, Barrie & Jenkins, 1973.

Potpourris and Other Fragrant Delights, Jacqueline Heriteau, Penguin, 1978

The Herb and Spice Book, Sarah Garland, Frances Lincoln, 1979

Household Self-Sufficiency, Jackie French, Aird Books, Melbourne, 1994

Women in Roman Britain, Lindsay Allason Jones, British Museum Publications, 1989

The National Trust Manual of Housekeeping, Allen Lane, 1984

INDEX

ACKNOWLEDGEMENTS

Author's acknowledgements
The author wishes to thank the following people for their help and support during the creation of this book: Erica Kelly; Rose and Graham White; Jonathan, Orlanda, and Morwenna Baylis.

Publisher's acknowledgements
Gaia Books would like to thank the following for their help in the production of this book: Stuart and Binny, Mich and Alastair, and Caroline (assistance on location), Sarah English (the best bed and breakfast), Rachel Jukes (photography styling assistance), Caroline Burraway, Tony Boylan and Robert Burns (paint effects and photography assistance), Sheila and Derek Mathews, Andrew Ross-Hunt at House Points, Jo Godfrey Wood (props) and Helen Spencer (props and scanning), Patrick Furse, Phil Gamble ((design assistance,) Lynn Bresler (index), Lesley Gilbert (copy management) and especially to the author, Beverly, and her family for the free run of their house during photography shoots and for their good humour, sustenance, and generosity.

Also published by Gaia Books

The Feng Shui Handbook
How to create a healthier living
and working environment
Master Lam Kam Chuen
£12.99
ISBN 1 85675 047 7

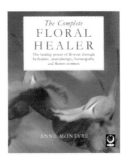

The Complete Floral Healer
A practical guide to the healing
power of flowers through
herbalism, aromatherapy,
homeopathy and flower essences
Anne McIntyre
£15.99
ISBN 1 85675 067 1

The Rothschild Gardens
Miriam Rothschild, Kate Garton, Lionel de
Rothschild
Photography by Andrew Lawson
£25.00
ISBN 1 85675 092 2

H is for ecoHome
G is for ecoGarden (twin pack)
A to Z guides to a healthy
house and a healthy garden
Anna Kruger/Nigel Dudley & Sue Stickland
£3.99 (twin pack)
ISBN 1 85675 030 2/ISBN
185675 035 3

The Natural Garden Book
Gardening in harmony with
nature
Peter Harper, Jeremy Light and Chris
Madsen
Hardback £18.99
ISBN 1 85675 085 X
Paperback £14.99
ISBN 1 85675 056 6

The New Natural Family Doctor
The authoritative self-help guide to
health and natural medicine
Dr Andrew Stanway
£12.99
ISBN 1 85675 057 4

To request a full catalogue of titles published by Gaia Books please call 01453 752985, Fax 01453 752987
or write to
Gaia Books Ltd.,
20 High Street, Stroud, Gloucestershire, GL5 1AS
e-mail address gaiabook@star.co.uk
Internet address www.bookshop.co.uk/Gaiabooks